COMPUTE!'s QUICK & EASY GUIDE TO dBase III Plus™

Chuck Doherty

COMPUTE!™ Publications, Inc. abc
Part of ABC Consumer Magazines, Inc.
One of the ABC Publishing Companies
Greensboro, North Carolina

Printed in the United States of America

10 9 8 7 6 5 4

ISBN 0-87455-107-2

COMPUTE! Publications, Inc., Post Office Box 5406, Greensboro, NC 27403, (919) 275-9809, is part of ABC Consumer Magazines, Inc., one of the ABC Publishing Companies, and is not associated with any manufacturer of personal computers. IBM is a registered trademark of International Business Machines. *dBase III Plus* is a trademark of Ashton-Tate.

Table of Contents

Foreword

COMPUTE!'s Quick and Easy Guide to dBase III Plus is your reference and learning tool for Ashton-Tate's *dBase III Plus,* the software monument which helped make the IBM PC the industry standard. It handles astronomical quantities of data in thousands of offices across the country.

COMPUTE!'s *Quick and Easy Guide to dBase III Plus* not only covers high-powered business applications, but also reveals another side to *dBase. Anyone* who needs to keep important information—membership records for a club or church, a class roster, a Christmas-card list, or any other collection of information—can take advantage of the power of *dBase.* You can quickly set up *dBase* to manage essential data without having to learn a programming language, without having to be a computer expert.

COMPUTE!'s Quick and Easy Guide to dBase III Plus starts with a tutorial on the commands and what they do. It contains a command summary complete with examples. You'll learn how to arrange a database and display your information the way you want it, how to make reports and mailing labels from your information, and how you can integrate *dBase* with *Lotus 1-2-3* and *WordStar* files to prepare impressive reports.

You'll keep *COMPUTE!'s Quick and Easy Guide to dBase III Plus* beside your computer for quick reference and to help you grow in expertise.

Chapter 1
Introduction

Chapter 1
Introduction

This book serves as a companion to *dBase III Plus*. The extensive documentation provided with *dBase III Plus* gives a much more detailed explanation of the program's commands and functions, but can make it difficult to find a simple answer to a question. *COMPUTE!'s Quick and Easy Guide to dBase III Plus* is for those who want to begin using the program quickly and for experienced users who need help in a hurry.

The book is organized to give you quick and easy answers to commonly asked questions, such as "How do I add records to a file?" or "How do I find a specific record that I know is in there somewhere?" In addition, *COMPUTE!'s Quick and Easy Guide to dBase III Plus* includes hints and tips not found in the manual. This will make using the program even more simple.

Although *dBase III Plus* includes a powerful programming language, this book will not cover programming in the *dBase III Plus* language. Instead, we'll concentrate on how you can get the most out of *dBase III Plus* as an operator of its built-in programming. You will gain full control of its powerful features and commands.

To get the most from *dBase III Plus,* you should be familiar with the basics of computer operation. You should have a good working knowledge of the disk operating system (DOS), and be comfortable with basic DOS operations: directories, file management, copying, and the like. The DOS manual supplied with your computer will answer most of the questions you might have about DOS operations.

The Story of *dBase III Plus*

In 1980, microcomputers were becoming commonplace in business applications. Because the available software was poor—much of what was available was riddled with bugs and limitations—there was clearly a need for flexible, high-quality business software that would take advantage of the rapid advance in hardware technology that was taking place. When the Ashton-Tate corporation began marketing *dBase II* later that year, computer users found a product they could trust and soon adopted it as the most popular choice in information-management software.

In 1981, IBM introduced the IBM Personal Computer and Ashton-Tate soon followed with *dBase III*, a natural extension of *dBase II* that included many new features to take advantage of the capabilities of this new generation of hardware.

dBase III's powerful programming language made the program the choice of many professional developers and programmers. They helped make *dBase III* and the IBM PC the industry standards they are today.

In 1985, Ashton-Tate again took the software world by storm with *dBase III Plus*, the latest version of what had already become an industry standard. With built-in support for networks and dozens of new features, *dBase III Plus* clinched the title of being the most popular data-management program for the IBM PC and the growing list of compatible computers. Its unique mix of easy operation and powerful language make it appealing to everyone from novice to professional programmer.

Version 1.1 of *dBase III Plus* was introduced in 1986. In this latest version, Ashton-Tate improved customer relations by removing the copy-protection from the product. In earlier versions, the copy-protection system made it impossible to make backup copies of the program disks themselves and to put the program on a hard disk. Registered owners of *dBase III Plus* Version 1.0 can upgrade to this new version for a nominal charge. If you are using an earlier version, by all means take advantage of the upgrade offer.

What Is *dBase III Plus*?

dBase III Plus is a sophisticated information-management or database program. But what does that mean, and how does it differ from the hundreds of other products on the market? Each of the other programs touts its own features and benefits.

In their simpler forms, data-management programs can be used to record names and addresses, telephone numbers, or any other information which would normally be kept on paper and stored in a filing system. Even the most Spartan data-management program allows you to store records to a floppy disk and recall them as needed. In addition, the program is certain to provide a means of printing and displaying information from the file, perhaps sorted in some predefined order.

A more sophisticated data-management program will allow you to create customized screen displays for entering and viewing the information in your files. In addition, these programs will let you sort and select records according to more complex criteria, giving you the ability to produce a more detailed report. For example, you could print a list of clients who meet several criteria—those who live in a certain state, who have not ordered from you for three months, and who are engaged in a specific business.

With *relational* databases such as *dBase III Plus,* you can optimize your record keeping by linking information in one data file to that in another. For example, you could keep customer information (names, addresses, and so forth) in one file, and corresponding records for customer purchases in another. By linking the files, you will have access to all of the information, along with a dramatic increase in storage efficiency and speed.

The most sophisticated relational data-management programs, such as *dBase III Plus,* include a programming language which allows you to predetermine the operation of the database by creating *command files.* These are programs which allow you to tailor *dBase III Plus* to exactly fit specific applications. Programs written in this way allow inexperienced users to operate the program easily, since the users are isolated from the actual commands given to the computer itself.

Who Should Use *dBase III Plus*?

If you have a task that requires the collection, storage, and processing of information, you will benefit from *dBase III Plus.* Typical uses for the program include:

- mailing-list management
- marketing research
- inventory management
- accounting and billing professional time
- manufacturing cost control
- job costing
- expense tracking
- and much more

Despite its power, *dBase III Plus* is a program with which users of all levels of proficiency can be comfortable. The basic concepts of the program are easy to understand, and once you are accustomed to these, more complex operations become easier to grasp. Before looking at *dBase III Plus* in detail, let's review some of the concepts that are common to every computerized data-management system.

Data-Management Fundamentals

To understand computerized data management, it helps to visualize a manual system. Consider a simple name-and-address file. More often than not, it is in the form of a card file—when you add a name, you simply add a new card to the file. To find someone's telephone number or address, you flip through the file until you reach the appropriate card. The principles of electronic data management are not far removed from those used in manual systems; in fact, much of the terminology is the same as well.

Figure 1-1. How a Database Is Like a Card File

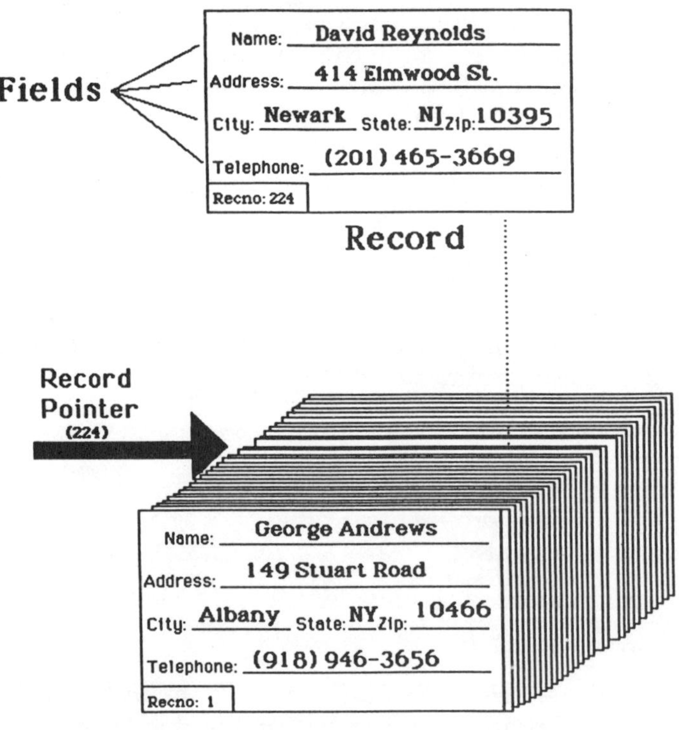

In a paper-and-pencil filing system, each individual name and address has its own card. The computerized equivalent of this card is called a *record.* A collection of records, in turn, comprises a *file.* These may be names and addresses (as in the example in Figure 1-1), inventory information, sales transactions, or any other kind of information. Instead of being written on paper, the records are stored on a magnetic disk for faster retrieval. A file can hold a single record or several thousand, depending on how much room is available on the disk.

Each record is made up of one or more *fields,* with each storing a specific piece of information. If we were computerizing our name-and-address file, we would have a field for name, one for address, another for city, and so on. A record in a computerized system has a unique number, called the *record number,* which is assigned sequentially when the record is added. The first record placed in a file is record 1, the second is 2, and so on.

When we flip through the cards in our desktop card file, we look at only one record at a time, perhaps using our finger as a pointer to the current record. The same holds true for a computerized system; even though there may be hundreds or thousands of records present, only one is the active record—the one we are currently examining. Instead of a finger, we need a method of marking a record as the current one. This is done by the *record pointer,* a part of the system that indicates which record is currently being processed.

Any command we issue (such as Display, Edit, or Delete) affects the record indicated by the pointer. It is almost as though we took that particular card from the manual file and placed it on the desk in front of us. Just as we would put one card away and take out another in order to make changes to it, we move the pointer from record to record to select the ones we wish to view or modify.

dBase III Plus gives you many powerful techniques for locating, displaying, and modifying records in the file. As we go on, you'll see how easy it is to create a file, add and modify records, and produce reports based on the information in a file. You'll also see how *dBase III Plus* can be used for many common business applications, including mailing-list management, expense tracking, and more.

Chapter 2
System Requirements

Chapter 2

System Requirements

By anyone's standards, *dBase III Plus* is a sophisticated program which places demands on hardware.

Ashton-Tate recommends an IBM PC, PC XT, or PC AT (or true compatible) with a minimum of 256K of memory and two 360K floppy disk drives. This bare-bones configuration, however, is both slow and difficult to use for a number of reasons.

dBase III Plus uses the disk drive for almost every operation. Data is stored on disk and loaded into memory when it is being examined or modified. Moreover, parts of the *dBase* program itself reside on disk and load into memory when needed during operation. Because of this, the speed of your computer's disk drives has a profound effect on the speed of operation of *dBase III Plus*.

Hard Disks

Using a hard-disk drive rather than a floppy drive makes a dramatic difference in the performance of *dBase III Plus*. Not only is a hard-disk drive many times faster than a floppy, its storage capacity is typically 30–60 times greater than that of a standard floppy disk. This allows you to create and manipulate larger data files and keep all of your work in one central location.

Extra Memory

Increasing memory to the maximum of 640K recognized by DOS also helps *dBase III Plus* to improve its performance. Larger memory capacity allows faster operation, since data being transferred between disk and memory can be held in temporary storage until it is needed. In addition, extra memory allows you to use other programs in conjunction with *dBase III Plus*. These additional programs may include an external text editor used for programming, or many of the popular memory-resident programs (such as *Sidekick* or *Superkey*) which can simplify a number of tasks.

Depending on what computer you are using, adding more memory may involve simply plugging chips onto the main circuit board, or it may require the addition of another circuit board or *card*. The latter is the case with a standard IBM PC. Many multifunction cards are available for these machines which provide additional memory up to 640K. Some of these cards also include clock/calendar circuitry for automatic date- and time-stamping of files. Most of these boards include serial and parallel interfaces, game-port adapters, and software for using these new features.

Recent price reductions for both RAM and hard-disk drives make these options less of a luxury than they were previously. Twenty-megabyte hard-disk drives that fit almost any IBM-compatible computer are available for well under $400, and sets of nine 64K RAM chips are commonly priced for under $20. Multifunction boards with a full complement of memory are available for less than $200.

If you are handy enough to change a faucet washer, you can easily install a hard disk and additional memory. Anyone who wants to get the most from *dBase III Plus* should have hard-disk storage and at least 512K of memory. Expanding the memory to 640K is best.

Faster Processors

If your application is very demanding, consider using a computer based on the 80286 microprocessor. These include the IBM PC AT or the Compaq Deskpro 286. These computers offer much better performance than machines such as the IBM PC or PC XT that use the older 8088 processor. Not only is the actual processing speed faster, but the disk read/write performance of these machines is much better as well. This makes a tremendous difference when using heavily disk-dependent programs such as *dBase III Plus*.

Monitors

dBase III Plus works with either a monochrome or color monitor. If you use the program with a color display, you have full control over the color selection. Many users choose this option because they can design applications with error messages and prompts displayed in special colors. When used with a monochrome monitor, *dBase III Plus* allows you to display data with bright, normal, or inverse letters (white letters on a black background), and to underline. Many users find monochrome monitors easier to read and gentler on their eyes when used for extended periods.

Printers

Almost any printer, whether it is dot-matrix or letter-quality, will work with *dBase III Plus*. Some features, however, make a great deal of difference in how easy they are to use. Make certain that the printer you select is capable of handling pin-fed, continuous-form paper, and does not require single sheets which are fed in by hand, sheet by sheet. If you plan to produce complex reports with many columns of information, you may need a wide-carriage printer which can support 14-inch-wide paper.

Try to select a pin-feed printer with paper-tractor mechanisms which slide fully left and right. Many machines do not allow you to move the left and right pin-feed wheels closer than eight or nine inches from each other. While this is not a concern when using ordinary paper for reports or general printing, it does present a problem when using mailing labels which are one label wide on the sheet, or Rolodex-style cards which may require the pins to be no more than three or four inches apart.

For most users, any of the midpriced, dot-matrix printers from major manufacturers such as Epson, Panasonic, Okidata, or IBM will provide good performance. If, however, you plan to subject your printer to periods of heavy or continuous use, or will rely on the machine for the operation of your business, don't settle for anything less than a rock-solid machine. Consider the printer's speed and durability when making your decision. A slow or unreliable printer can be the Achilles heel of an otherwise fine computer system.

One final consideration: If you must choose between a parallel or serial interface for your printer, choose the parallel to avoid compatibility problems. Almost every quality printer today is available with a standard parallel interface, and few machines even offer the choice of a serial interface.

Installing *dBase III Plus*

dBase III Plus comes with an automatic installation routine that makes it easy to load the program onto your computer. Hard-disk users should create a separate subdirectory (such as

\DBASE) and install the program files in this directory.

The first time you run *dBase III Plus* Version 1.1 you will be asked to enter your name, your company name, and the product's serial number (found on the original disk label). This information is then recorded and displayed onscreen each time you start the system. The older version of the program (1.0) does not have this sign-on feature and relies on copy-protection for program security. The "Getting Started" section of the *dBase III Plus* manual covers the installation process in detail.

A file called CONFIG.DB is created in the same subdirectory as the program files during the installation procedure. When *dBase III Plus* starts, it looks for this file and takes its initial setup instructions from there. In a later section, we'll discuss how to modify this file to customize *dBase III Plus* for your needs.

Once the program is installed, you should create a DOS batch file which changes directories and starts the program with a single command. A typical DOS batch file would look like this:

```
ECHO OFF
CD \DBASE
DBASE
CD \
```

If you are not familiar with how to create and use DOS batch files, consult the DOS manual provided with your computer.

Chapter 3

How to Use *dBase III Plus*

Chapter 3

How to Use *dBase III Plus*

Like any other program, *dBase III Plus* is entered through the computer's operating system (DOS). If using a floppy disk–based system, put the program disk in drive A. If you have a hard-disk system, make certain you are currently in the same directory as your *dBase III Plus* program files. At the DOS prompt, type DBASE; the program will start and display its opening screen. Unless you tell it to do otherwise, *dBase III Plus* will automatically go into the Assistant operating mode.

The Assistant is a system of menus and prompts which will guide you through most commands and operations. You can specify whether or not the Assistant appears at startup by modifying the contents of the system configuration file. In a later section, you'll see how to use this file to set operating conditions to suit your taste. To leave the Assistant and reach the command level of *dBase,* simply press the Esc key. (Type ASSIST at a command-level prompt to restart the Assistant mode.)

Always use the QUIT command to exit from *dBase III Plus* before shutting off the computer. The QUIT command leaves *dBase III Plus* and returns to DOS, safely closing any open files in the process. If you simply shut the computer off while *dBase III Plus* is operating, you take the chance of damaging files and losing data.

dBase III Plus Operating Modes

You can interact with *dBase III Plus* at a number of levels. The most sophisticated mode of operation is the use of the system under the control of a program written in the *dBase* language. Here, your actions and the responses of *dBase III Plus* are controlled by instructions contained in a program file that was created by an experienced programmer. (When you look at a *dBase* directory, this type of file will have the extension PRG.) Programs written in this way are easy for novice and casual users to operate, but require the initial, time-consuming task of creating, testing, and installing the program files. In addition, operating in this mode prevents direct access to many *dBase* features.

Another option is to use the *dBase III Plus* Assistant system. Almost every *dBase* command is available through the Assistant, and many users choose this mode for everyday operation. However, once you are familiar with the commands of *dBase III Plus*, the Assistant is of little use.

At the command level, instructions are given to the program by typing them directly at the *dBase* prompt—a period character on the command line, called the *dot prompt*. At first, you may feel that having nothing more than a dot on the screen waiting for you to type a command seems less than inviting, but after working with *dBase* for a few days, you'll be comfortable with using the command line to operate the program.

Entering and Editing Commands

See Chapter 5 for a complete list of *dBase* commands. These commands can be entered on the command line in either lowercase or uppercase letters. A command will not be executed until you press the Enter key, which allows you to first edit the command using the backspace and cursor arrow keys. Press Enter only when the command is exactly as you want it.

dBase III Plus uses the same cursor-movement and editing commands as *WordStar*, the well-known word processing program. If you are comfortable with *WordStar*, working with *dBase III Plus* will be easy. The following list shows some of the commands available to you:

Ctrl-T	Remove the word to the right of the cursor.
Ctrl-Y	Remove an entire line.
Ctrl-S	Move the cursor one character to the left.
Ctrl-A	Move the cursor one word to the left.
Ctrl-D	Move the cursor one character to the right.
Ctrl-F	Move the cursor one word to the right.
Del	Remove the character at the cursor.
Backspace	Remove the character to the left of the cursor.

dBase III Plus has a history feature. It stores the last 20 commands just as they were entered on the command line and allows you to call them back to the screen as needed. This makes it easier to repeat a command or correct a mistake, since you do not have to type the command again. Pressing the up-arrow (↑) key moves back through the prior commands, while pressing the down-arrow (↓) key moves ahead to bring up the more recently entered commands.

Getting Help

If you type a command that is incorrect for some reason, *dBase* will respond with an error message which will help you to determine the cause of the problem. Typing the following command will generate such an error:

LOCATE FAR FIRSTNAME = "FRED"

dBase responds with:

Syntax Error
?
LOCATE FAR FIRSTNAME = "FRED"
Do you want some help? (Y/N)

After indicating that this is a syntax error (an error in the spelling or format of a command), *dBase* displays the offending command and places a question mark above the part of the command that caused the error. In this case, the word FAR was used instead of the proper command FOR. By showing the exact location of an error, *dBase III Plus* makes the mistake easier to find and correct.

The message *Do you want some help? (Y/N)* allows you to summon a help screen showing the proper use of the command. Pressing any key other than Y at this point will return you to the dot prompt.

From the command level, *dBase III Plus* can be used with different levels of help and prompting. Pressing the F1 function key or typing HELP at the dot prompt presents a menu of help topics from which you can get more detailed information.

You can specify whether *dBase* will respond to command errors with offers of help, as it did in the above example. The commands SET HELP ON and SET HELP OFF control this aspect of the program's response.

Canceling a Command

Pressing the Esc (escape) key prior to hitting Enter will remove a command from the command line. Esc can also be used to stop most commands during execution. For example, typing LIST instructs *dBase* to display on the screen every record in a file. If the file you are using is very large, this could take some time. Pressing the Esc key anytime during this process will cancel the listing and return to the dot prompt immediately.

The commands SET ESCAPE ON and SET ESCAPE OFF can be used to control use of the Esc key, but for most applications, ESCAPE should be set to ON, allowing you to interrupt commands when necessary.

The Status Bar

The status bar, an information feature of *dBase III Plus*, is a one-line summary which appears near the bottom of the screen. It shows the current disk drive, the name of the file you are using, the number of records, the current position of the record pointer, and several other bits of information including the settings of the Insert, Caps Lock, and Num Lock keys. (See Figure 3.1.) The commands SET STATUS ON and SET STATUS OFF control whether or not the status bar is displayed.

Figure 3-1. The *dBase III Plus* Status Bar

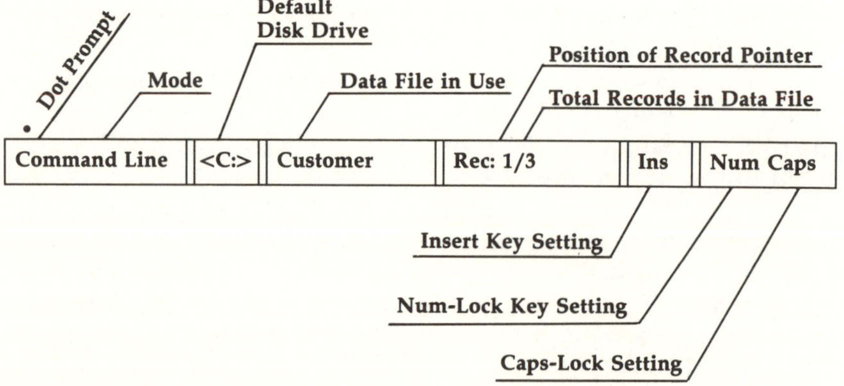

Checking the System Status

A more detailed report on system status is available by typing DISPLAY STATUS which brings a full description of system information to the screen. (See Figure 3-2.) At the top of this display, you'll see a list of data files currently in use, along with any open index, format, and view files (more on these later). In addition, you'll see the current default disk drive, file search path, print destination, printer left-margin setting, and active work area.

Below this, the status display screen shows the current setting (either ON or OFF) of the many SET commands used in *dBase III Plus*. These commands will also be covered in detail further on.

Finally, the status screen shows the current settings of the nine programmable function keys. The F1 function key is always dedicated to summoning help, but function keys F2–F10 can be programmed as desired, allowing you to invoke commonly used commands with a single keystroke instead of typing them in their entirety. Some machines have these keys located at the left of the keyboard; others position them along the top, above the number keys.

Figure 3-2. The System Status Screen

```
Currently Selected Database:
Select area: 1.  Database in Use: C:customer.dbf  Alias: CUSTOMER

File search path:
Default disk drive: C:
Print destination: LPT1:
Margin = 0
Current work area = 1

ALTERNATE  - OFF  DELETED     - OFF   FIXED      - OFF  SAFETY     - ON
BELL       - OFF  DELIMITERS  - OFF   HEADING    - ON   SCOREBOARD - ON
CARRY      - OFF  DEVICE      - SCRN  HELP       - ON   STATUS     - OFF
CATALOG    - OFF  DOHISTORY   - OFF   HISTORY    - ON   STEP       - OFF
CENTURY    - OFF  ECHO        - OFF   INTENSITY  - ON   TALK       - ON
CONFIRM    - ON   ESCAPE      - ON    MENU       - OFF  TITLE      - ON
CONSOLE    - ON   EXACT       - OFF   PRINT      - OFF  UNIQUE     - OFF
DEBUG      - OFF  FIELDS      - OFF

Programmable function keys:
F2  - assist;
F3  - list;
F4  - MODI COMM
F5  - MODI COMM UTILITY;
F6  - USE
F7  - MODI COMM MAIN;
F8  - DO MAIN;
F9  - append;
F10 - CLOS ALL;
```

Creating Files

At the heart of *dBase III Plus* is the data file itself, where all of the information is held. As described earlier, each file is a collection of records, and each record is a collection of fields. In *dBase III Plus*, a record can contain as many as 128 fields, and a file can contain an almost unlimited number of records; the system will address up to *one billion* records. You are likely to run out information to record (or out of memory to hold the information) long before you exceed the capacity of *dBase III Plus*.

Spending a few minutes thinking about your overall goal prior to creating a data file will save much frustration later on. Your first approach to a data-storage problem may not be the most efficient solution. A properly designed data file should give you the room to store the information you need, but not waste storage space with redundant data or empty fields.

Filenames

Data filenames are subject to the same naming conventions that affect all DOS files: Filenames can be from one to eight characters in length (although unlike DOS, *dBase III Plus* does not allow the single letters *A–J* alone to be used for filenames. They may contain any combination of letters, numbers, or the underscore character. Eight characters may not seem like a lot, but with proper planning it is possible to give your data files very informative names. Blanks and most special characters (@, #, &, %, =, –, and so on) are not allowed.

Each of the following is a valid *dBase III Plus* data filename:

CUSTOMER
PARTS_01
INVOICES
PEOPLEA
PEOPLEB

The following are invalid filenames, for the reasons given:

OPEN_ORDERS	too long
WEEK 2	contains a space
FILE=3	contains an invalid character (=)

When you look at a *dBase III Plus* directory, you will see that it assigns the extension .DBF to all database filenames.

Field Names

Within each record, *dBase III Plus* field names can be up to ten characters in length, must begin with a letter, and can contain letters, numbers, or the underscore character. Blank spaces are not permitted in field names, but the underscore character permits you to create names which are more descriptive than a collection of letters. For example, the name CUSTNUM for a customer-number field is not as informative as CUST_NUM, although both are valid field names.

Each of the following is a valid *dBase III Plus* field name:

ITEM
PRICE_EACH
DATE_IN
F_NAME
DESCRIP
SCORE_21

The following are not valid as field names, for the reasons given:

CUSTOMER_NAME	too long
1ST_CALL	begins with a number
HOME PHONE	contains a space
BALL&CHAIN	contains an invalid character (&)

Field Types

Each field in the *dBase* record structure must be assigned a particular type. The available types are as follows:

Character fields. This is the most commonly used type in *dBase III Plus* because character fields can be used for almost every storage task. They can be 1–254 characters in length, and can store any letter of the alphabet (upper- or lowercase), numbers, symbols such as $, %, &, and #, and punctuation marks.

Use character fields for names, addresses, item descriptions, and any other collection of letters or numbers. Character fields are also best for data which, although in numeric format, is not used for mathematical calculations. For example, phone numbers and zip codes should both be stored in character rather than numeric fields.

The length that you specify for a field is important. Fields must be long enough to hold the data that they need to hold, yet short enough to conserve disk space and memory. The amount of space occupied by a *dBase III Plus* record depends on the number of fields, the field type, and the length of each field. If a length of 50 is chosen for a character field, that field occupies 50 bytes in every record, regardless of the number of characters actually stored in the field for a particular entry. If you use this 50-byte field to store a part number that never exceeds eight characters in length, a considerable amount of disk space will be wasted. Of course, you wouldn't want to make a field so short that it would not hold the data you need to store. A good rule of thumb is to make the length of a character field 1 or 2 bytes longer than the longest value you ever plan to store in it.

Numeric fields. These may be 2–19 digits long, with up to nine decimal places of precision. Data held in a numeric field may be used in any type of mathematical calculation.

When creating numeric fields which include decimal places, keep in mind that the decimal point itself occupies one character of the total field length. For example, a numeric field with a total length of 7 is required to store a value as high as 9999.99 (four bytes for the integer portion of the number, one for the decimal point, and two for the decimal places).

As with character fields, the length that you choose for a numeric field should not be so small that it will restrict your operations, but also should not be so long as to waste storage space.

Logical fields. These always occupy only one byte of storage. The value held in the field is considered to be either true or false, but the value of the field can be entered by typing either *F*, *N*, or *n* for false, or *T*, *Y*, or *y* for true.

Logical values are typically used to store a yes-or-no fact about a field, such as whether or not a person's club membership is current, or whether or not an item is a special order. A useful convention when using logical fields is to name them so that the field name poses a question that the value in the field answers. For example, a field for indicating whether or not an invoice was paid could be named IS_PAID. A True in this field would answer *yes* to the question "Has this Invoice been paid?"

Date fields. These are always eight bytes in length and can store any valid date. *dBase III Plus* checks the validity of dates as they are entered into a date field, preventing you from entering impossible dates such as 02/30/87 or 13/01/85. Attempting to enter an invalid date results in an error message.

Dates can be processed much like numeric data. By subtracting dates, you can calculate the number of days between them. In addition, you can add or subtract integers from dates in order to calculate what the date will be a certain number of days in the past or future.

Memo fields. A unique feature of *dBase III Plus* is its ability to hold large amounts of text associated with a particular record in a special type of field: the memo field. When entering or editing a record with a memo field, moving the cursor to the memo field and pressing Ctrl-PgDn brings you into a full screen where you can write as much or as little text as you wish, all of which is stored along with that record. Pressing Ctrl-PgUp finishes the operation and returns you to the main part of the record.

Inside a memo field, the program operates much like a word processor. It allows you to insert or delete text, move from line to line, and edit the text as required. The commands used by the *dBase III Plus* word processor are similar to those used by *WordStar*.

When memo fields are used, *dBase III Plus* creates a separate file (a .DBT file) which holds the memo data. This arrangement allows more efficient use of disk storage, since memo fields are only as long as the data you actually keep in them. In other types of fields, a fixed amount of storage space is occupied by each field, regardless of its contents.

Memo fields have limitations that should be considered before using them. Most importantly, you cannot search a memo field to locate information stored there. This makes a memo field useful only for holding notes about a given record. Secondly, memo fields are difficult to use under program control and are hard to format during printout.

Creating a File

Using a list of names as an example, let's create a simple file to hold this information. We are going to create a small data file called PEOPLE, so at the *dBase* dot prompt, type CREATE PEOPLE. This tells *dBase* to make a data file, and use PEOPLE as the name.

dBase III Plus next presents a Create File Screen, with a help menu at the top explaining the available commands. Like most *dBase III Plus* help menus, this display can be turned on or off by pressing the F1 (help) key.

At this point, *dBase III Plus* is awaiting the name of the first field in your data file, so type LAST (since this field will store last names) and press Enter.

Next, *dBase* needs to know what kind of field is required for this information. The default selection, Character, appears in the Type section, but can be changed to whatever field type is desired. Press the space bar, and note that the field type changes from Character to Numeric. Press it again, and it changes to Date, then Logical, and finally Memo. Another press of the space bar returns the field type to Character, the type required for this data. Pressing Enter at this point accepts Character as the field type. You are then prompted for the field length.

We want to provide enough room for a typical last name, but don't want to waste space by allowing more characters than are ever likely to be used. For our example file, let's use a field length of 10 characters, which should accommodate most names.

Since this is not a numeric field, *dBase* does not ask for the number of decimal places. *dBase* is now ready for the second field description. Enter FIRST as the field name, accept Character as the type by pressing Enter in the Type section, and give this field a length of 10 as well. For field 3, the middle name, use MI as the name, Character as the type, and 2 as its length.

When *dBase* is ready for field 4, simply press Return without entering a field name. This signals *dBase* that no more field names will be entered. When prompted *Press Enter to Confirm, any other key to Resume,* press Enter once again. *dBase* will next ask if you wish to input data records into this new file. Answer by pressing Y.

You'll now see a blank record presented in the upper-left corner of the screen. Type *Francis* in the LAST field and press Enter; the cursor will move to the FIRST field. Type *Robert* and press Enter once more. Now enter *M* as the middle initial and press Enter again.

Record 1 is completed and stored in the file. *dBase III Plus* is now ready for record 2. Enter records 2–11 from the following list:

Last	**First**	**MI**
Jones	Allen	F
Baker	Susan	G
Adams	Karen	R
Williams	David	Y
Randall	Fred	U
Stuart	George	S
Kennedy	Victor	E
Martin	Steven	D
Davis	Pat	V
Carson	William	K

After entering record 11 (when *dBase III* is ready for record 12), press Escape to return to the dot prompt. The data file is now ready and will be used in later examples of locating and sorting records. Be sure to close the file (by typing either USE, CLOSE DATABASES, or QUIT) when you are through.

Chapter 4

Adding and Editing Data

Chapter 4

Adding and Editing Data

In most data-management applications, you will create and maintain a number of different data files. In order to work with the file you want, you need some way to list the data files currently on your disk. Within *dBase III Plus*, the DIR command gives a listing of data files and shows the number of records in each, the date of last update, and the size of the file in bytes (Figure 4-1). Used alone, DIR shows only those files that end with the file extension .DBF, which identifies them as *dBase* data files.

Figure 4-1. A *dBase* Directory Screen

```
. dir
Database Files     # Records   Last Update   Size
STOCK.DBF               51     01/04/86      3504
VENDORS.DBF              4     01/04/86       987
ITEMS.DBF                6     01/04/86       858
PEOPLE.DBF              11     03/27/86      1326
NEWPEOPL.DBF            10     03/27/86      1229
INV_LI.DBF               2     09/20/86       282
VENDLINK.DBF            16     04/08/86       307
CUSTS.DBF                5     09/20/86      1201
TENO_LI.DBF              0     09/20/86       258
INVOICE.DBF              2     09/20/86       542
TEST.DBF                51     10/24/86      3739
   14233 bytes in 11 files.
1888256 bytes remaining on drive.
```

The *dBase III Plus* DIR command can also be used much like the DOS DIR command, in that it can be followed by the *wildcard characters* * and ?. The * character can represent any combination of characters, and ? can represent any single character. Typing DIR *.* shows a listing of all files on the current disk or directory; DIR *.NDX lists only those ending with the extension NDX, and so on. The DOS manual supplied with your computer explains how to use these wildcards in more detail.

Working with a File

Once a data file exists, there are a number of ways to add records or to change the information which is already stored in a record. Before performing any operations on a file, it is necessary to open the file. The *dBase* command USE, followed by the filename, is used to open a data file. For example, you must type USE PEOPLE at the dot prompt in order to use the PEOPLE file.

When you are finished working with a file, typing USE by itself (with no filename) closes the active file. Always remember to close a file before you turn the computer off.

Adding Records

Once a file is open, you can add new records with the APPEND command. Typing APPEND at the dot prompt places you into the full-screen editing mode, positioned on a blank record. This new record will have a record number one higher than the current last record in the data file. After filling in the desired information, press Ctrl-End. This adds the new record to the data file and returns you to the dot prompt.

You don't have to return to the dot prompt to add yet another new record. Press Return while your cursor is on the last field of a new record. *dBase III Plus* will accept the record and present a new, blank record to be filled out. When you have finished entering all new records you want to add, simply press Ctrl-End. If you instead press Esc at this point, *dBase* will exit to the dot prompt without adding the last record you typed in.

Looking at Records

An important part of using any database program is the ability to view records once they have been entered. With *dBase III Plus*, you have extensive control over the format in which information is displayed—both onscreen and on paper.

The simplest method of displaying information is by using the DISPLAY command. Entered alone, DISPLAY shows the contents of the current record—the one at which the record pointer is positioned. There are many variations to the DISPLAY command:

DISPLAY ALL

shows all of the records in the file. Adding the optional OFF parameter:

DISPLAY ALL OFF

shows all the records, but omits the record number.

DISPLAY NEXT 10

shows ten records beginning with the current record.

DISPLAY NAME, ADDRESS

shows the contents of the NAME and ADDRESS fields in the current record. This can be combined with ALL, as in

DISPLAY ALL NAME, ADDRESS

to show the contents of these fields in all records.

DISPLAY FOR NAME = "DAVE SMITH"

shows any records in the file which have DAVE SMITH in the NAME field. Note the use of quotation marks around the information used as the search pattern. This is necessary whenever searching for character-field information.

Any of the above commands can be followed with the words TO PRINT to route the information to the printer rather than to the screen. *dBase* has a powerful report generator which gives you much more control over printed output, but sending information to the printer with a DISPLAY or LIST command is a quick way to get a printout.

The DISPLAY command differs from LIST in that information is displayed one screenful at a time: When the screen is full, DISPLAY prompts you to press a key for the next screen of information. LIST displays information continuously, and does not pause when the screen is full. Use LIST when sending information to the printer; DISPLAY is more useful when viewing information on the screen. A more detailed explanation of the DISPLAY and LIST commands can be found in chapter 5.

Moving the Record Pointer

Since the active record is indicated by the record pointer, it is important to know where the pointer is currently pointing, and how it can be moved to a desired record. To see the current position of the record pointer, use the RECNO( ) function.

? RECNO( )

The number of the active record will be reported. (See Figure 4-2).

Figure 4-2. Record-Pointer Commands

Record Pointer Commands

GO (or GOTO)

Used to position the record pointer to a specific record in the file.

EXAMPLE: The record pointer in this file is currently at record 4. The command GO 9 moves it directly to record 9.

Record Pointer (at record 4)

	LAST	FIRST	MI
1	Francis	Robert	M
2	Jones	Allan	F
3	Baker	Susan	G
4	Adams	Karen	R
5	Williams	David	V
6	Randall	Fred	U
7	Stuart	George	S
8	Kennedy	Victor	E
9	Martin	Steven	D
10	Davis	Pat	V
11	Carson	William	K

After the command GO 9.

Record Pointer (at record 9)

	LAST	FIRST	MI
1	Francis	Robert	M
2	Jones	Allan	F
3	Baker	Susan	G
4	Adams	Karen	R
5	Williams	David	V
6	Randall	Fred	U
7	Stuart	George	S
8	Kennedy	Victor	E
9	Martin	Steven	D
10	Davis	Pat	V
11	Carson	William	K

GO TOP Moves the record pointer to the first record in the file.

Record Pointer (at record 1)

	LAST	FIRST	MI
1	Francis	Robert	M
2	Jones	Allan	F
3	Baker	Susan	G
4	Adams	Karen	R
5	Williams	David	V
6	Randall	Fred	U
7	Stuart	George	S
8	Kennedy	Victor	E
9	Martin	Steven	D
10	Davis	Pat	V
11	Carson	William	K

GO BOTTOM Positions the record pointer to the last record in the file.

Record Pointer (at record 11)

	LAST	FIRST	MI
1	Francis	Robert	M
2	Jones	Allan	F
3	Baker	Susan	G
4	Adams	Karen	R
5	Williams	David	V
6	Randall	Fred	U
7	Stuart	George	S
8	Kennedy	Victor	E
9	Martin	Steven	D
10	Davis	Pat	V
11	Carson	William	K

Several commands can set the record pointer anywhere you want it. The most direct method of moving the record pointer is by using the GOTO or GO commands. For example, to position the pointer to record number 15 in order to view or modify that record, you would enter

GOTO 15

In fact, *dBase III Plus* allows you to move the record pointer to a specific record number simply by typing the record number and pressing Enter. For example, entering 25 alone has the same effect as entering GOTO 25.

To move the pointer to the first record of a file, you could enter GOTO 1, or simply type

GO TOP

Moving to the bottom of a file is just as easy. Simply enter

GO BOTTOM

and the record pointer will be positioned on the last record in the file.

To move the record pointer one or more records at a time, use the SKIP command. Alone, SKIP increases the record pointer by one.

? RECNO( )
15
SKIP
? RECNO( )
16

If you follow SKIP with a number, such as SKIP 3, the record pointer will be moved forward by that number of records. Following the SKIP command with a negative number moves the record pointer backwards (to lower-numbered records).

? RECNO( )
18
SKIP −2
? RECNO( )
16

Attempting to SKIP or GOTO a record number which is not in the file results in the error message *Record is out of range.*

The record pointer can also be moved to a particular record by using the LOCATE command. LOCATE, along with FIND and SEEK, is used to find records which satisfy certain criteria. These commands are discussed in more detail in the section devoted to locating records.

Deleting Records

When a record within a database is no longer needed, *dBase III Plus* allows you to remove it from the file. The DELETE command removes single or multiple records depending on how the command is used.

To remove a single record, place the record pointer on the record you wish to remove and enter

DELETE

An alternative is to specify the record number in the DELETE command, to insure that the proper record is removed

DELETE RECORD 12

Like the DISPLAY command, DELETE can be enhanced with options to make it operate more easily. For example, you may wish to remove all of the records from a mailing-list file where the address is in New York. An easy way to do this is

DELETE FOR STATE = "NY"

DELETE does not actually remove records from the data file; it merely marks them in such a way that they are ignored. *dBase III Plus* allows you to decide whether or not you want to use records marked for deletion by using the SET DELETED ON/OFF command. Entering SET DELETED ON causes deleted records to be ignored by subsequent commands. For all practical purposes, the file behaves as though the deleted records did not exist. Entering SET DELETED OFF, on the other hand, includes deleted records in most operations. If a record is marked for deletion, an asterisk (*) appears to the left of the record when it is displayed or listed. *Del* will appear on the status bar during editing operations.

If you change your mind about deleting a record, you can RECALL it back into the file. The RECALL command follows the same syntax as the DELETE command, but its effect is just the opposite. In order for the RECALL command to have an effect, the deleted records must first be made accessible with SET DELETED OFF.

When you wish to remove deleted records permanently, the PACK command will purge them from the file and recover the disk space the deleted records previously occupied. Once you PACK a file, deleted records are gone forever, so make certain that the records that you have marked for deletion really are ones you do not want.

Changing Data

When the record pointer is on a record you wish to modify, typing EDIT will bring the record onscreen and allow you to change any of the information in the record. The cursor arrow keys allow you to move from field to field, making whatever changes may be necessary. *dBase III Plus* provides a help menu at the top of the screen showing which keys to use for moving through the record and for editing data. This menu (like all *dBase III Plus* help menus) can be turned on and off by pressing F1.

Once the record is modified as desired, pressing Ctrl-End saves the edited record in the file and returns you to the dot prompt.

While in the editing mode, you can use the PgUp and PgDn keys on the numeric keypad to move forward and backward in the file one record at a time. This makes it possible to change a group of records with one EDIT command. If you use the PgUp or PgDn key, you may modify records just as if you had used the EDIT command for each record.

In some cases, you may wish to limit your changes to certain fields or to prevent particular fields from being visible during the editing process. To do this, follow the EDIT command with FIELDS and a list of the fields you wish to have displayed and made available for change. For example,

EDIT FIELDS NAME, SS_NUM

EDIT can also be used to position the record pointer on the desired record, as in

EDIT RECORD 47

The Browse Mode

The BROWSE command gives you an alternative to editing one record at a time. When in the browse mode, records are displayed one per line, in what is often called *table format.* This display looks and operates much like an electronic spreadsheet such as *Lotus 1-2-3*. Each record occupies a row, and each field of a record appears in an individual column within the row. Up to 17 records can be viewed at once in this mode.

While in this mode, you can move the cursor from record to record (row to row) by pressing the up-arrow and down-arrow keys. The PgUp and PgDn keys show you one screenful at a time, moving through the file forward or backward, respectively. The Home and End keys move from field to field within a record, and the right- and left-arrow keys move the cursor within a field itself. Pressing Ctrl together with the right- or left-arrow keys scrolls the record across the screen, bringing other fields into view. Function key F1 turns on and off a navigation menu if help is needed. Pressing Esc or Ctrl-W at any time leaves the browse mode and returns you to the dot prompt.

Any changes made to records while in browse mode are recorded in the file, just as if you were working in the full-screen editing mode.

Pressing the F10 function key brings up a browse menu with a number of options (discussed in detail in Chapter 5). These allow you to skip to a particular record, freeze part of the record onscreen, or limit your changes to only one field.

It's easy to delete or recall records while in browse mode; simply place the cursor anywhere on the row of a record you wish to delete or recall and press Ctrl-U. When the cursor is on a record which has been marked for deletion, the word *Del* will appear at the top of the screen (or in the status bar at the bottom of the screen if STATUS is set ON). Depending on the setting of the SET DELETED command, records which have been marked for deletion will or will not appear within browse mode.

Scrolling past the end of the file while in browse mode gives you the option of APPENDing additional records. In some file designs, especially those with a limited number of fields, this is a very convenient way to add new records.

Format Files

The default screen in the edit mode presents the record in the upper left-hand corner of the screen with each field identified by name. While this may be fine for many operations, it does not present the most attractive form, nor does it make information entry easy for inexperienced users.

You may custom design your own screen to use for information entry. The Format Screens option allows you to display the fields in the exact place on the screen you wish, and to use prompts and field descriptions of your own choosing. In addition, screen formats can be defined to display single- and double-line boxes around your data, making it stand out for easy reading. A number of screen formats can be created and used (one at a time) with a single database. In this way, you can control the amount of information that is available to each user and can provide different levels of access to the information.

dBase III Plus provides two methods of creating and editing screen formats. One is the CREATE SCREEN command. This places you into a full-screen mode in which you can move the fields to the desired position on the screen and can enter text for use as prompts and field descriptions. To create a screen called PARTS to be used with the data file called ITEMS, you would enter the following command at the dot prompt:

USE ITEMS
CREATE SCREEN PARTS

When you exit the CREATE SCREEN mode, *dBase III Plus* produces a screen-format file with the name you specified and with the extension .FMT. This file (PARTS.FMT) is activated by entering

SET FORMAT TO PARTS

After this, when you edit the file ITEMS, you will do it with the screen format defined by the format file PARTS. You may also use the Assistant to create your own .FMT file. When in the Assistant menu, just cursor down to the *Format for Screen* choice and enter the screen format name.

A second and more versatile method of creating and modifying screen formats is to create the format file directly. The command

MODIFY COMMAND <format filename>.FMT

creates a format file with the specifed name, and places you into the *dBase III Plus* program editor. In this mode, you are able to create programs and format files as you would with a word processor. Format files recognize only a limited number of commands: @ *row,col* SAY; @ *row,col* GET; and @ *row,col* TO *row,col*. These commands will be covered in detail below.

Before designing a format file it is necessary to understand how *dBase III Plus* addresses the screen. The *dBase* screen is divided into rows and columns of text. The standard IBM monitor (either monochrome or color) has 25 horizontal rows of text, each 80 characters in length. The rows are numbered from the top, beginning with row 0 and extending to row 24 at the bottom. Likewise, columns are numbered 0–79, going from left to right. To position text or data at a particular location on the screen you must specify both the row and column at which you want the information displayed. For example, to make the word *Hello* appear near the middle of the screen, you would enter the following at the dot prompt:

@ 12,40 SAY "Hello"

To display the literal string of letters and not the contents of a data field, quotes were added around the word *Hello*.

Similarly, information from data files can be positioned onscreen, either with the @ *row,col* SAY command (which merely displays the information) or with the @ *row,col* GET command (which allows editing and modification of the information).

For example, you may want to prompt the user for a customer number, which is stored in our data file in the field CUS_NUM. To do this within a format file, include the following commands:

@ 8,21 SAY "Enter Customer Number:"
@ 8,48 GET CUS_NUM

Obviously, this will be much more informative to the operator than the default edit mode which simply displays the field name CUS_NUM.

SAY and GET commands can be combined, eliminating the need for calculating the exact column in which the GET should be positioned:

@ 8,21 SAY "Enter Customer Number: " GET CUS_NUM

This locates the GET directly after the information presented by the SAY.

The command: @ *row,col* TO *row,col* DOUBLE allows you to dress up your format screens by drawing boxes around sections of the screen. The command draws a box between a specified upper left and lower right corners. Adding the optional command DOUBLE draws the box with double lines. To draw a double-line box near the top of the screen, you would enter

@ 2,5 TO 6,75 DOUBLE

A box has no effect on other information on the screen, unless that information lies in the path of the lines of the box.

This allows you to enter text inside boxes or draw boxes around existing information.

Combining these commands, a typical format file may look like this:

```
@ 2, 5 TO 6,75 DOUBLE
@ 4,31 SAY "Customer Information"
@ 8, 5 TO 20,75
@ 10,15 SAY "Last Name: " GET LAST
@ 10,51 SAY "First Name: " GET FIRST
@ 12,17 SAY "Address: " GET ADDRESS
@ 14,20 SAY "City: " GET CITY
@ 14,48 SAY "State: " GET STATE
@ 14,59 SAY "Zip code: " GET ZIP
@ 16,15 SAY "Telephone: " GET PHONE
```

Controlling Data Entry with the PICTURE Clause

dBase offers an extensive array of features to control the information which is displayed with a SAY or a GET, and the information which can be typed by the user in response to a GET. The PICTURE and RANGE commands control both the acceptable limits of data and the format in which it is shown.

A picture clause is comprised of the command PICTURE, followed by a string of characters enclosed in quotes. Each character in this string, if it is a valid picture symbol, has an effect on the character at the same position within the expression used with the SAY or GET. In other words, in a five-character picture string, the first character in the string affects the first character in the expression, the second affects the second, and so on.

The exclamation point is used to convert lowercase letters to uppercase. This symbol is often used along with a GET to force the letters in certain fields to uppercase. In the format file above, the following command could be used to keep all entries in the STATE field in uppercase:

```
@ 14,48 SAY "State: " GET STATE PICTURE "!!"
```

Whenever any letters are typed into this field, they will appear and be stored as uppercase, regardless of whether they were entered as upper- or lowercase. Since the picture template ("!!") is only two characters in length, it restricts entry into the field to two characters as well, even if the defined field length were longer.

Mixing picture-template symbols allows us to affect different characters in the same field. For example, to GET a value into a ten-character-wide field called LASTNAME, and insure that the first character is always entered as uppercase, mix the ! template symbol with the symbol X, which allows input of any character:

@ 10,15 SAY "Enter last name: " GET LASTNAME PICTURE "!XXXXXXXXX"

Another example of using picture templates is to format telephone numbers to the standard style of (area code) phone number:

@ 16,15 SAY "Telephone: " GET PHONE PICTURE "(999) 999-9999"

The 9s in this picture template allow only numbers to be typed in; hitting any other character when entering information in this field will have no effect. The parentheses and hyphen are not picture-template symbols, and will be included with the information recorded in the field. If no data is entered into the field however, the field is left blank and the hyphen and parentheses are not recorded.

With numeric fields, the picture clause controls both the length of the field and the position of the decimal place. To display a field called PRICE with a comma after the thousands place and with two decimal places, you would use the following:

@ 10,15 SAY PRICE PICTURE "#,###.##"

Symbols available for use in picture templates include:

9 Accept only digits for character data, or digits and signs (+/−) for numeric entries.
Accept only digits, blanks, and signs.
A Accept only alphabetic letters.
L Accept only logical data.
Y Accept only logical Y or N; automatically convert input to uppercase.
! Force lowercase letters to uppercase.
X Accept any character.

In addition to picture-template symbols (which affect a single character within the SAY or GET), *dBase III Plus* also provides *picture functions* (picture commands beginning with

@). These functions affect the entire expression. Picture functions allow you, for example, to force an entire expression or field into uppercase with a single command, regardless of the expression's length. Consider a 20-character field called NAME which contains a mixture of upper- and lowercase characters. To display this field with all of the characters in uppercase, you could use ten picture-template symbols:

@ 10,15 SAY NAME PICTURE "!!!!!!!!!!!!!!!!!!!!"

However, you can achieve the same result with a single picture function:

@ 10,15 SAY NAME PICTURE "@!"

Not all picture functions have a template counterpart. For example, the @Z function causes a numeric value which evaluates to zero to be displayed as a blank, rather than as a zero. There is no way to achieve the same result with picture-template symbols alone.

A few other picture functions are:

@C Display CR (credit) following a positive number.
@X Display DB (debit) following a negative number.
@(Show negative numbers within parentheses.
@B Display numbers left-justified.

You can combine picture functions with each other, or with picture templates, for even more flexibility. For example, to create a three-digit-wide, left-justified, numeric entry field with zeros shown as blanks, you would use the following:

@ 10,15 SAY "Price Each: " GET PRICE PICTURE "@ZB ###"

Here, the Z function blanks zero values, the B forces left-justification, and the three #s limit the entry to three numbers. Notice the space between @ZB and ###; this is required when combining picture functions and templates in the same expression.

The RANGE Option

A further option available with numeric and date fields is the RANGE clause. RANGE allows you to specify acceptable upper and lower limits for data. If an entry falls outside these limits, an error message is displayed and the information must be reentered.

RANGE is useful to screen out mistakes on the part of the operator. For example, you may be recording gasoline purchases in an automotive expense file. It is unlikely that a gas purchase will be for less than $1.00, or for more than $50.00. RANGE can verify that the entry is within these limits:

@ 15,30 SAY "Enter Amount: " GET GAS_COST PICTURE "##.##" RANGE 1,50

With dates, RANGE can verify that an entry is between set limits. To prompt for a date entry which must fall between January 1, 1980 and the present, you would use the RANGE clause in this way:

@ 10,15 SAY "Membership Date: " GET MEM_DATE RANGE CTOD("01/01/80"),TODAY( )

The *dBase III Plus* TODAY( ) function returns the current date as held in the computer's clock/calender. If your computer does not have a built-in realtime clock, you must enter the values during boot-up, prior to beginning *dBase III Plus*. If you don't, this function will not operate properly.

Changing Multiple Records

Occasionally it is necessary to change many or all of the records in a file in some way. The REPLACE ALL command allows you to do this quickly and easily.

Consider a file of inventory information holding model number, manufacturer, quantity on hand, and price. If one manufacturer, for example Acme Inc., raises the price of their products by 10 percent, you can change the amount stored in the PRICE field for all appropriate records with the following single command:

REPLACE ALL PRICE WITH PRICE *1.1 FOR MANUFACT = "Acme Inc."

This command has two main sections; the first part, REPLACE ALL PRICE WITH PRICE *1.1, tells *dBase* to replace the contents of the field PRICE with the current value multiplied by 1.1, which represents a 10-percent increase. The latter part of the command, FOR MANUFACT = "Acme Inc.", restricts the changes to records which contain Acme Inc. in the MANUFACT (manufacturer) field. Many other *dBase III Plus* commands also use FOR and WHILE clauses to restrict their effect to only certain records within a given field.

Memory Variables

Memory variables are temporary storage areas within *dBase III Plus* that are used to hold the results of calculations, information used when updating a database, and information which is passed to and from the operator. Each memory variable has a name, a type (character, numeric, logical, or date), and a value.

dBase III Plus allows up to 256 memory variables to be active at any one time. Each can be up to 256 characters in length, but the total space available for memory variables is limited to 6000 bytes. If more memory-variable space is required, it can be specified in the CONFIG.DB file (see the *dBase III Plus* manual for more information on this feature).

Creating Memory Variables

The simplest way to create a memory variable is with the STORE or = command. For example, to create a character-type variable called NAME containing the name Peter Smith, you would issue the command:

STORE "Peter Smith" TO NAME

or

NAME = "Peter Smith"

Since Peter Smith is a character string, *dBase III Plus* knows to make NAME a character variable.

To see the current value of a variable, type a question mark and the variable name. *dBase III Plus* will respond with the current value of that variable.

? NAME
Peter Smith

Numeric variables work the same way. To create a variable called ON_HAND which stores the total number of items in the field COUNT in an inventory file, use the following commands:

USE INVENTORY
SUM COUNT TO ON_HAND

To examine the value of this variable, enter

? ON_HAND
35

Logical variables can hold only true (.T.) or false (.F.) values. If the value assigned to a memory variable is a logical .T. or .F., then *dBase III Plus* will make the variable involved a logical variable. For example,

STORE .T. TO IS_MEMBER

creates a logical variable called IS_MEMBER, and assigns a true value to it. Note the use of IS_ as part of the variable name, which identifies the variable as a logical variable. *dBase III Plus* does not require you to use the IS_ format for logical variable names, but it does make the variable more understandable to the user. In this case, the value of IS_MEMBER answers the question "Is this person a member?" A logical true means yes, they are a member, and a false value means they are not.

Date variables are like date fields, and can be used for date arithmetic and tests. To create a date variable, the value you place in the variable must be of the date type.

STORE DATE( ) TO TODAY

will create a variable called TODAY containing the current system date. Remember that DATE( ) represents the value held in the operating system of the computer, and is accurate only if the system date was specified during start-up, or if the computer contains built-in clock/calendar hardware.

Storing a date that you enter from the keyboard to a memory variable requires that you change it from a character string to date format. To store the date July 8, 1954 into a date-type variable, use CTOD( ), the character-to-date conversion function:

STORE CTOD("07/08/54") TO DATE_1

The commands DISPLAY MEMORY and LIST MEMORY show a listing of all active memory variables, their type, and the current value of each:

DISPLAY MEMORY

```
NAME        pub  C  "Peter Smith"
ON_HAND     pub  N  35 (35.00000000)
IS_MEMBER   pub  L  .T.
TODAY       pub  D  04/03/87
DATE_1      pub  D  07/08/54
5 variables defined, 42 bytes used
251 variables available, 5958 bytes available
```

The *pub* notation (for *public*) means that a variable can be used and altered by any *dBase* program.

Saving Memory Variables for Later Use

Memory variables can be stored to files and recalled as needed. These files, which have the extension .MEM, follow the same naming rules as all DOS files.

To save all current memory variables to a file named STATUS, enter

SAVE TO STATUS

Occasionally, you need to save just one variable or a limited number of variables to a file. This is done with the SAVE ALL LIKE command:

SAVE ALL LIKE BIR_DATE TO DATES

This command will save the memory variable BIR_DATE in a file called DATES.

The wild-card characters * and ? can be used with the SAVE ALL LIKE command. This allows you to save a group of similar memory variables together. For example, if you had a variable called DATE_DUE, another called DATE_PAID, and another called DATE_OUT, you could save them together in a file called DATES.MEM with the following command:

SAVE ALL LIKE DATE* TO DATES

The asterisk represents any sequence of characters, of any length. Therefore, any variable beginning with the characters DATE, regardless of what follows, will be included.

Specified variables can also be excluded using the command SAVE ALL EXCEPT. If the command is entered in this way:

SAVE ALL EXCEPT DATE* TO NODATES

a file called NODATES.MEM is created which holds all of the active memory variables except those beginning with DATE.

Clearing Memory Variables

The RELEASE command cancels one or more memory variables. The command accepts either a list of memory variable names, or the ALL [LIKE/EXCEPT] clause. To release all of the memory variables beginning with DATE, issue the command:

RELEASE ALL LIKE DATE*

To remove all active memory variables from memory, enter

RELEASE ALL

Another way to do the same thing is to use the CLEAR MEMORY command.

Restoring Memory Variables

You can bring memory variables back from disk and make them available for use with the command

RESTORE FROM <filename> [ADDITIVE]

The <filename> is the name of the .MEM file in which the memory variables were put with a SAVE command.

When the RESTORE FROM command is executed, all of the memory variables which are currently active are normally released, and the variables in the file become the only memory variables that the system sees. By specifying the ADDITIVE option, memory variables which are currently active remain, and those in the file are made available as well.

Chapter 5

dBase III Plus Commands

Chapter 5

dBase III Plus Commands

This chapter guides you through the operation of the most commonly used *dBase III Plus* commands. The following list includes all of the commands described elsewhere in this book, but omits some advanced commands and those which are used exclusively by programmers.

Each command description consists of the command name, its application (Interactive, Program, or both Interactive and Program), and, when appropriate, an example of how the command is used.

Only the first four letters of each command need to be entered in most cases. For example, the command MODIFY STRUCTURE can be entered simply as MODI STRU to save time.

This holds true for the command keywords only, all other entries (such as field names or filenames) must still be typed in their entirety. To abbreviate the command DISPLAY LASTNAME,ADDRESS, the keyword DISPLAY could be shortened to DISP, but the field names LASTNAME and ADDRESS must be entered in full.

In this section, the following abbreviations will be used:

Symbol	**Definition**
< >	Indicates information which must be supplied by the user. The brackets themselves are not to be entered.
[ ]	Indicates information which is optional and need not be entered unless desired.
/	Indicates that the command can be used in more than one way. Enter only one of the command options found on either side of the slash.
<n>	A numeric expression. This could be a number, the contents of a numeric field, or the results of a calculation such as 2*2.
<c>	A character expression. This could be a literal string of characters enclosed in quotes, the contents of a character field, or any other type of character data.

<d> A date expression, such as the contents of a date field or a function that returns a date value.
<condition> A user-specified condition such as NAME="SMITH" or COST>=150.

?

Application

Interactive and Program

Syntax

? <expression>

Use

Shows the current value of <expression>, which may be a field name, memory variable, or any other expression with a numeric, character, date, or logical value.

Examples

? NAME
Bob Jones

? "NAME"
NAME

? 10*3
30

? IS_VALID
.T.

@

Application

Interactive and Program

Syntax

@ <*row,col*>
@ <*row,col*> SAY <expression>
@ <*row,col*> GET <field name/memory variable>

Use

@ *<row,col>* clears all or part of a single line of the screen display.
@...SAY displays text or data at a specified location on the screen or printer.
@...GET allows user input into data fields and memory variables.

SAYs and GETs can be used together or independently. PICTURE and RANGE clauses can be added to SAYs and GETs to control the type and length of data provided by the user.

Examples

@ 15,0

Clears all of row 15.

@ 20,40

Clears the right half of row 20.

@ 10,15 SAY ADDRESS

Displays the contents of data field ADDRESS on the screen at row 10, column 15.

@ 15,20 SAY "Enter your name: " GET NAME READ

Displays the prompt *Enter your name:* at row 15, column 20 and follows the prompt with an area where a value can be entered for the data field NAME. The READ command is required to activate the GET and allow user entry.

@ 15,35 GET STATE PICTURE "!!"
READ

The PICTURE clause (in this case, "!!") restricts the entry to two characters, and converts lowercase letters to uppercase.

@ 18,35 SAY "Enter Cost:" GET COST RANGE 10,100
READ

The RANGE clause restricts entry to a value between 10 and 100. Any entry outside this range will produce an error message.

@...TO

Application

Interactive and Program

Syntax

@ <*x*1,*y*1> [CLEAR] TO <*x*2,*y*2> [DOUBLE]

Use

Draws boxes around areas of the screen, or clears areas of the screen.

Examples

@ 10,20 TO 20,60

Draws a rectangular box onscreen from row 10, column 20 to row 20, column 60. The box is formed of single-line graphics characters.

@ 10,20 TO 20,60 DOUBLE

Draws a rectangular box onscreen from row 10, column 20 to row 20, column 60. The box is formed of double-line graphics characters.

@ 12,40 CLEAR

Clears the lower right corner of the screen, beginning at row 12, column 40 (midscreen).

@ 5,40 CLEAR TO 15,60

Clears the middle 20 columns of the screen (from column 40 to column 60) in the area between rows 5 and 15.

APPEND

Application

Interactive and Program

Syntax

APPEND [BLANK]

Use

Places you in a full-screen editing mode to enter new records. Filling in the fields and pressing Ctrl-W adds the new record to the end of the current data file and exits the editing mode. Pressing Enter on the last field in the record adds the record to the file and brings up another blank record for entry.

APPEND BLANK adds a blank record to the end of the current data file, but does not enter the full-screen editing mode. This command is usually used under program control where data is placed into the new record with the REPLACE command.

APPEND FROM

Application

Interactive and Program

Syntax

APPEND FROM <filename>

Use

Adds records to the currently active data file from the data file specified by <filename>. Only those fields which are common to both files are affected. By specifying a file type, you can use the APPEND FROM command to bring data from other software packages into *dBase III Plus.*

Examples

USE INVENTORY
APPEND FROM RECEIVING

Adds the records in the file RECEIVING.DBF to those already in the active file, INVENTORY.

USE MAILLIST
APPEND FROM OLDLIST FOR STATE = "NY"

Adds records from the file OLDLIST.DBF to those in MAILLIST. The optional condition (FOR STATE = "NY") means that only those records from OLDLIST in which the STATE field contains *NY* will be appended.

USE NAMES
APPEND FROM NEWNAMES.TXT TYPE DELIMITED

Bring data from the file NEWNAMES.TXT into the active data file. The data in NEWNAMES.TXT is assumed to be in an ASCII delimited format, with each field separated by commas and records separated by carriage returns. This format is a popular method of transferring data between different programs.

AVERAGE

Application

Interactive and Program

Syntax

AVERAGE <field(s)>

Use

Calculates the numeric average of the numeric values in the specified fields. The command affects all records in the file unless limited by some condition. The results of AVERAGE can be sent to a memory variable as well as displayed on the screen.

Examples

USE STOCK
AVERAGE COST
55 records averaged
COST
22.50

Shows that the average value of the field COST is $22.50.

AVERAGE COST FOR VENDOR = "ACME"
27 records averaged
COST
18.76

Shows that the average COST for records which contain *ACME* in the VENDOR field is $18.76.

AVERAGE COST TO AVCOST
55 records averaged
? AVCOST
22.50

BROWSE

Application

Interactive

Syntax

BROWSE [FIELDS <fieldlist>]

Use

Starts a full-screen editing and scanning mode with as many as 19 records visible on the screen at once (depending on whether MENU and STATUS are set OFF or ON). In this mode, records are presented one per row, much like a spreadsheet. The up- and down-arrow keys move the cursor from record to record, while the Home and End keys move between fields. Any changes you make to the data while in browse mode are recorded in the data file.

Browse allows you to specify the fields you wish included, and the desired order. Otherwise, BROWSE displays all of the fields in the file.

Pressing F10 brings into view the Browse Menu with the following options:

BOTTOM	Positions the record pointer on the last record in the file.
TOP	Positions the record pointer on the first record in the file.

LOCK	Prompts for a number which is then used to determine how many fields (counting from the left of the screen) will remain fixed in place at all times. This allows you to keep certain parts of a record in view while making changes to other fields.
RECORD NO.	Allows you to go to a specific record within the file.
FREEZE	Allows you to limit editing to a specified field.
FIND	Prompts for a value that is used to find a record based on the current index. (For indexed files only.)

CLEAR

Application

Interactive and Program

Syntax

CLEAR

Usage

Clears the display screen or a specific portion of the screen. CLEAR can be combined with the @ and TO commands to clear portions of the screen.

Examples

CLEAR

Clears the entire screen and positions the dot prompt at the bottom.

@ 2,10 CLEAR TO 15,20

Clears a rectangular area on the screen between row 2, column 10 and row 15, column 20.

@ 15,40 CLEAR

Clears the screen area below and to the right of row 15, column 40.

CLEAR ALL

Application

Interactive and Program

Syntax

CLEAR ALL

Use

Closes all open data files, their associated indices, and any open format and memo files. In addition, all memory variables are released and the active work area is reset to 1.

CLEAR MEMORY

Application

Interactive and Program

Syntax

CLEAR MEMORY

Use

Releases all currently active memory variables.

CLOSE

Application

Interactive and Program

Syntax

CLOSE <filetype> / ALL

Use

Closes all open files, or all files of a specified type. Memory variables are not affected.

Valid entries for <filetype> are:

ALTERNATE
DATABASES (also closes associated index and format files)
FORMAT
INDEX
PROCEDURE

Examples

CLOSE FORMAT

Closes the currently open format file. Any open data and index files remain unaffected.

CLOSE DATABASES

Closes all open data files, along with any associated index files and format files.

CLOSE ALL

Closes all open files regardless of type.

CONTINUE

Application

Program and Interactive

Syntax

CONTINUE

Use

Resumes the search for records specified by a LOCATE command. Since LOCATE finds only the first record matching a specified condition, CONTINUE is necessary to find subsequent matching records.

Example

USE INVOICE
LOCATE FOR INV_AMT >= 1000
Record = 20
CONTINUE
Record = 45
CONTINUE
Record = 71
CONTINUE
End of LOCATE scope.

COPY

Application

Interactive and Program

Syntax

COPY TO <filename>

Use

Copies all or part of the active database file to a new database file. Options allow you to restrict the records which are copied, or to limit the number of fields. COPY can also produce non-*dBase* files which can transfer data out of *dBase III Plus*.

Examples

USE PEOPLE
COPY TO FRIENDS

Creates a new data file called FRIENDS with the same information contained in the data file PEOPLE.

USE CUSTOMER
COPY TO NOREAST FOR STATE='MA' FIELDS NAME,ADDRESS,CITY,STATE

Creates a data file called NOREAST containing those records in the file CUSTOMER which have *MA* in the STATE field. The new file will contain only the fields NAME, ADDRESS, CITY, and STATE.

USE PEOPLE
COPY TO MAILLIST TYPE DELIMITED

Produces an ASCII file called MAILLIST.TXT containing the data found in PEOPLE.DBF. The new file will have fields separated by commas and quotes, and records separated by carriage returns. This format is a standard method of sharing information between different programs.

COPY FILE

Application

Interactive and Program

Syntax

COPY FILE <filename1> TO <filename2>

Use

Makes a duplicate of the file *filename1* with the name specified in *filename2.* Both *filename1* and *filename2* must include a complete filename, plus an extension if one is desired, and the drive and path if different from the current default.

Examples

COPY FILE MAIL.FMT TO ENTRY.FMT

Copies the file MAIL.FMT to a new file with the name ENTRY.FMT. The new file will be created on the current drive and path.

COPY FILE PEOPLE.DBF TO B:PEOPLE.DBF

Makes a copy of the data file PEOPLE.DBF with the same name, and places the new file on the disk in drive B.

COPY STRUCTURE

Application

Interactive and Program

Syntax

COPY STRUCTURE TO <filename> [FIELDS <fieldlist>]

Use

Creates a new, empty data file with the specified name. The new file has the same structure as the file currently in use. If the FIELDS option is used, the new file will contain only the fields listed in the field list.

Examples

USE MAILING
COPY STRUCTURE TO NEWMAIL

Creates an empty file named NEWMAIL.DBF with the same fields and structure as the active file MAILING.

USE MAILING
COPY STRUCTURE TO NAMES FIELDS LASTNAME,FIRSTNAME

Creates an empty file named NAMES.DBF from the structure of the file currently in use. Only two fields are included in the new file: LASTNAME and FIRSTNAME.

COUNT

Application

Interactive and Program

Syntax

COUNT [<condition>]

Use

Counts the records in the data file which match the optional specified condition. If no condition is specified, all of the records in the file are counted.

Examples

USE STOCK
COUNT
51 records

USE STOCK
COUNT FOR PRICE >=100
13 records

Indicates the number of records in the file having an entry equal to or greater than 100 in the numeric field PRICE.

CREATE

Application

Interactive

Syntax

CREATE <filename>

Use

Creates a new *dBase III Plus* data file. This command places you into a full-screen file design mode where you specify the various fields, along with their type and length, for the new file. Unless otherwise specified, the extension .DBF will be added to the filename.

See the discussion of creating files in chapter 3 for more detail.

CREATE LABEL

Application

Interactive

Syntax

CREATE LABEL <filename>

Use

Used to design a label-format file. The command starts a full-screen label editor controlled by a menu. The label file created by this command is activated with the LABEL FORM command.

For more information, see discussion of label design in chapter 8.

CREATE REPORT

Application

Interactive

Syntax

CREATE REPORT <filename>

Use

Used to design a report-format file. The command starts a full-screen report editor controlled by a menu.

For more information on the report design process, see chapter 8.

CREATE SCREEN

Application

Interactive

Syntax

CREATE SCREEN <filename>

Use

Used to design a screen-format file which controls screen layout during full-screen operations such as EDIT or APPEND. The command starts a full-screen report editor controlled by a menu. The screen-format file created in the screen design process is activated with the SET FORMAT TO <filename> command.

DELETE

Application

Interactive and Program

Syntax

DELETE [WHILE <condition>] [FOR <condition>]

Use

Marks the specified record or records for deletion. Records marked in this way remain in the data file until purged with the PACK command.

Examples

DELETE

Marks the current record—the one indicated by the record pointer—for deletion.

DELETE FOR COST<=50

Marks for deletion any records in the file in which the numeric field COST holds a value less than or equal to 50.

DELETE REST

Marks for deletion all records from the current record to the end of the file.

DIR

Application

Interactive

Syntax

DIR [<skeleton>]

Use

Displays a listing of and information about the files on the current disk drive. Unless otherwise specified, only database (.DBF) files are listed. The filename, number of records, date of last update, and size in bytes are shown for each file.

If a data file is currently in use, the DIR command may not show an accurate count of the number of records in the active file. The command reads the file header for a record count, which is only updated when a file is closed. To see how many records are in the active file, use the DISPLAY STRUCTURE command.

Examples

DIR

```
Database Files   # Records   Last Update   Size
STOCK.DBF            10        04/05/87     838
PEOPLE.DBF           11        04/05/87     886
1724 bytes in 2 files.
7294976 bytes remaining on drive.
```

Shows all of the data files on the current drive.

DIR *.*

```
DBASE.EXE      ID.EXE       CONFIG.SYS  INITDB.BAT  INSTALL.BAT
DBASEINL.OVL   DBASE.MSG    HELP.DBS    DBASE.SER   ASSIST.HLP
DBASE.OVL      NE.COM       CONFIG.DB   STOCK.DBT   STOCK.FRM
STOCK.DBF      PEOPLE.DBF   ITEM.NDX
611842 bytes in 18 files.
7294976 bytes remaining on drive.
```

Lists all of the files on the default drive and path.

DISPLAY

Application

Interactive and Program

Syntax

DISPLAY [<fields>] [<condition>]

Use

Shows the contents of a record or series of records. Display differs from LIST in that it pauses for a keypress after displaying 20 records, making it easier to view records on the screen.

Examples

DISPLAY

Shows the contents of the current record.

DISPLAY NEXT 5 TO PRINT

Lists on the printer the contents of the current record and the four following records.

DISPLAY FOR STATE = "MA" FIELDS LASTNAME, FIRSTNAME

Lists the contents of the LASTNAME and FIRSTNAME fields for all records in which the STATE field contains *MA*.

DISPLAY HISTORY

Application

Interactive

Syntax

DISPLAY HISTORY

Use

Shows the last series of commands that were typed at the dot prompt. The most recent commands will appear at the bottom of the list, and those occurring before will appear above them. The up- and down-arrow keys can be used from the dot prompt to bring these commands back for reentry.

Example

DISPLAY HISTORY
LIST
EDIT
DISPLAY NEXT 10
DIR

Shows that the most recently entered command was DIR, preceded by DISPLAY NEXT 10, EDIT, and LIST.

DISPLAY MEMORY

Application

Interactive

Syntax

DISPLAY MEMORY [TO PRINT]

Use

Shows the name, type, and value of all currently active memory variables. The amount of space available for memory variables and the amount already in use are also shown.

Example

DISPLAY MEMORY

```
DATE1   pub   D   04/05/87
DATE2   pub   D   05/05/87
DATE3   pub   D   06/04/87
NAME    pub   C   "Bob Jones"
PRICE   pub   N   123 (        123.00000000)
  5 variables defined, 47 bytes used
  251 variables available, 5953 bytes available
```

DISPLAY STATUS

Application

Interactive

Syntax

DISPLAY STATUS [TO PRINT]

Use

Shows the current status of the *dBase III Plus* operating system. The name and work area of all open data files are indicated; active index files and their key expression, open format files, and active views and filters are shown. In addition, the status report indicates the setting (ON or OFF) of the various environmental settings (SET commands) and the current string assigned to each of the ten function keys.

Example

DISPLAY STATUS

```
Currently Selected Database:
Select area:  1,  Database in Use:  B:people3.dbf  Alias: PEOPLE3
      Master index file:  B:firstnam.ndx  Key:  FIRST

File search path:
Default disk drive: B:
Print destination:  PRN:
Margin =   0
Current work area =   1

ALTERNATE - ON    DELETED - OFF      FIXED - OFF        SAFETY - ON
BELL - OFF        DELIMITERS - OFF   HEADING - ON       SCOREBOARD - ON
CARRY - OFF       DEVICE - SCRN      HELP - ON          STATUS - OFF
CATALOG - OFF     DOHISTORY - OFF    HISTORY - ON       STEP - OFF
CENTURY - OFF     ECHO - OFF         INTENSITY - ON     TALK - ON
CONFIRM - ON      ESCAPE - ON        MENU - OFF         TITLE - ON
CONSOLE - ON      EXACT - OFF        PRINT - OFF        UNIQUE - OFF
DEBUG - OFF       FIELDS - OFF

Programmable function keys:
F2   assist;
F3   list;
F4   dir;
F5   display structure;
F6   display status;
F7   display memory;
F8   display;
F9   append;
F10  edit;
```

DISPLAY STRUCTURE

Application

Interactive

Syntax

DISPLAY STRUCTURE [TO PRINT]

Use

Shows the field names, types, and sizes for the records of the currently active data file. Also indicates the number of records and the date that the file was last updated.

Example

USE STOCK
DISPLAY STRUCTURE
Structure for database: C:STOCK.DBF
Number of data records: 10
Date of last update: 04/05/87

Field	Field Name	Type	Width	Dec
1	ITEM_NO	Character	7	
2	TYPE	Character	10	
3	DESCRIP	Character	22	
4	COUNT	Numeric	4	
5	MIN	Numeric	4	
6	MAX	Numeric	4	
7	COST	Numeric	6	2
** Total **			58	

EDIT

Application

Interactive and Program

Syntax

EDIT [FIELDS <field list>]

Use

Starts a full-screen editing mode in which the contents of a record can be changed as needed. If a format file is active, the layout of the screen is taken from information in the format file.

In the EDIT mode, the arrow keys move from field to field, and PgUp and PgDn move from record to record within the file. Pressing Ctrl-End or Ctrl-W saves the changes and exits the edit mode. Pressing the Esc key exits the edit mode without saving changes to the currently displayed record.

EDIT is identical to CHANGE.

EJECT

Application

Interactive and Program

Syntax

EJECT

Use

Issues a form-feed command to the printer, causing the sheet of paper currently in place to be ejected, and the next sheet to be aligned with the top of form. Use EJECT after printing information to reset top-of-form and to remove the printed data without misaligning the printer.

ERASE

Application

Interactive and Program

Syntax

ERASE <filename.extension>

Use

Deletes the specified file from disk. The entire filename including extension must be specified. Active files cannot be deleted. If the file to be erased is not on the current drive or directory, you can specify the complete drive and pathname.

Examples

ERASE NAMES.DBF

Deletes the data file NAMES from the current (default) disk drive.

ERASE B:ZIP.NDX

Deletes the index file ZIP from drive B.

FIND

Application

Interactive and Program

Syntax

FIND <character string>

Use

Locates a character string in the indexed field of the active database. This command requires that the file in use be indexed and that the index is active.

Examples

USE PEOPLE INDEX LASTNAME
FIND SMITH
Record = 25

USE STOCK
SET INDEX TO TYPE
FIND TRASHCAN
No Find

GO/GOTO

Application

Interactive and Program

Syntax

GO <n>/TOP/BOTTOM
GOTO <n>/TOP/BOTTOM

Use

Positions the record pointer to the record number specified by <n>. GO TOP and GO BOTTOM move the record pointer to the first or last records in the data file, respectively.

Examples

USE PEOPLE
GO 4
? RECNO( )
4

GO BOTTOM
? RECNO( )
11

GO 100
Record is out of range

HELP

Application

Interactive

Syntax

HELP [<keyword>]

Use

Brings a menu of help topics to the screen. Selecting any of the menu choices presents more detailed help about the chosen subject. If a <keyword> is specified along with HELP, a screen of information specific to that command is displayed. Pressing the Esc key exits the HELP mode.

From the dot prompt, pressing function key F1 is the same as typing a HELP command.

Examples

HELP

Displays the HELP menu.

HELP QUIT

Displays a screen of information about the QUIT command.

INDEX

Application

Interactive and Program

Syntax

INDEX ON <key> TO <filename>

Use

Creates an index (.NDX) file which controls the order of the current data file. Records in the data file will appear in the order established by <key>, most often a field in the data file. For more detailed information on the INDEX command, see the discussion of controlling record order in chapter 7.

Example

USE PEOPLE
INDEX ON LASTNAME TO LAST

Creates an index file called LAST.NDX which will organize the current data file (PEOPLE) in order according to the contents of the field LASTNAME.

LABEL FORM

Application

Interactive and Program

Syntax

LABEL FORM <filename> [WHILE <condition>] [FOR <condition>] [TO PRINT] [SAMPLE]

Use

Activates a label-format file previously created with the CREATE LABEL or MODIFY LABEL commands. See chapter 8 for more information on printing labels.

Example

USE PEOPLE
LABEL FORM MAILING FOR STATE = "NY" TO PRINT SAMPLE

Prints labels from data in the active database file, using the format specified in the label-format file MAILING.LBL, including only records from the active file in which the STATE field contains *NY.* A set of sample labels are printed and printing pauses prior to the actual label printing to verify label alignment in the printer.

LIST

Application

Interactive and Program

Syntax

LIST [<field list>] [WHILE <condition>] [FOR <condition>] [TO PRINT]

Use

Displays the contents of the data file to screen or printer. LIST is similar to DISPLAY ALL, except the display does not pause when the screen is filled.

Example

USE STOCK
LIST NEXT 3

Record#	ITEM_NO	TYPE	DESCRIP	COUNT	COST
1	F0220	BAIT	CATFISH-20 OZ.	17	5.62
2	B6700	BALL	BOWLING BALL-16 LB.	4	19.95
3	C1201	COMPRESSOR	1/2HP RAND	1	932.74

LOCATE

Application

Interactive and Program

Syntax

LOCATE <condition>

Use

Searches the current data file for the first record which matches the specified condition. Unless limited in some way, the command begins its search at the first record in the file and continues until a match is found or until the end of the file is reached. LOCATE finds only the first record that matches the specified condition. To find subsequent matching records, use the CONTINUE command.

Examples

LOCATE FOR NAME = "Bob Smith"
Record = 5

Indicates that record 5 is the first record of the file containing the character string *Bob Smith* in the NAME field.

LOCATE REST FOR MODEL_NUM = "JS-45"
End of Locate Scope

Indicates that no record between the current position of the record pointer and the end of the file contains *JS-45* in the MODEL_NUM field. The REST causes LOCATE to begin at the current record rather than at the beginning of the file.

MODIFY LABEL

Application

Interactive

Syntax

MODIFY LABEL <filename>

Use

Used to modify an existing label-format file. The command starts a full-screen label design editor controlled by a menu. For more information, see discussion of label design in chapter 8.

MODIFY REPORT

Application

Interactive

Syntax

MODIFY REPORT <filename>

Use

Used to modify an existing report-format file. The command starts a full-screen report design editor controlled by a menu. The report design process is described in detail in chapter 8.

MODIFY SCREEN

Application

Interactive

Syntax

MODIFY SCREEN <filename>

Use

Used to modify existing screen-format files, which control screen layout during full-screen operations such as EDIT or APPEND. The command starts a full-screen format editor controlled by a menu.

MODIFY STRUCTURE

Application

Interactive

Syntax

MODIFY STRUCTURE

Use

Allows changes to the structure of the current database file. New fields can be added, and existing fields can be modified or deleted altogether. This command places you into the same full-screen file-design mode provided for the CREATE command.

Before modifying the existing database, the command makes a copy with the current structure. This copy will have the extension .BAK. The modified database file will still have whatever filename and extension (usually .DBF) that the original file had.

See the discussion of creating files in chapter 3 for more detail.

PACK

Application

Interactive and Program

Syntax

PACK

Use

Removes all those records from the active data file which have been marked for deletion with the DELETE command, and recovers the disk space those records formerly occupied. After the file is packed, all active indices are automatically rebuilt.

Setting TALK to ON gives a more informative view of what is happening during the PACK process by showing how many records have been packed and how much of the file has been reindexed.

QUIT

Application

Interactive and Program

Syntax

QUIT

Use

Closes all open data files and indices and exits *dBase III Plus.* Always issue the QUIT command to leave *dBase III Plus* prior to shutting the computer off.

READ

Application

Interactive and Program

Syntax

READ [SAVE]

Use

Causes *dBase* to ask for data through an @...GET command.

Example

```
STORE "    " TO NAME
@10,15 SAY "What is your name: " GET NAME
  PICTURE "@!"
READ
```

Places a blank, highlighted input area on the screen following a prompt at row 10, column 15, and places the cursor inside the highlighted area. The user can provide input by typing in the highlighted area. Input ends when the Enter key is pressed. The input is then stored in the memory variable NAME.

RECALL

Application

Interactive and Program

Syntax

RECALL ALL/<condition>

Use

Reactivates records which were previously marked for deletion with the DELETE command. This command works only before a PACK command is performed. Once the file is packed, deleted records cannot be recovered. The SET DELETED command must be OFF for RECALL ALL to work. With DELETED ON you must specify individually the records you wish recalled.

Examples

RECALL

Recovers the current record.

RECALL ALL

Recovers all records which have been marked for deletion since the last PACK.

RECALL NEXT 25

Reinstates any records in the next 25 which have been marked for deletion.

RECALL RECORD 45

Brings record number 45 back into the file.

REINDEX

Application

Interactive and Program

Syntax

REINDEX

Use

Rebuilds all active index files for the current data file. Use this command if you suspect that the index files may be corrupted, or if the data files were modified in any way without the index files being active. If TALK is set ON, *dBase III Plus* will inform you of its progress during the REINDEX process.

Example

USE PEOPLE INDEX LASTNAME,ZIP
REINDEX
Rebuilding index - LASTNAME.NDX
156 Records indexed
Rebuilding index - ZIP.NDX
156 records indexed

RELEASE

Application

Interactive and Program

Syntax

RELEASE <mem variable list>

Use

Releases the specified active memory variables, making the space they formerly occupied available for new variables. (See also CLEAR MEMORY.)

Examples

RELEASE DATE1

Releases the memory variable named DATE1.

RELEASE ALL LIKE DATE*
Releases all memory variables which begin with DATE.

RELEASE ALL
Releases all memory variables.

RENAME

Application
Interactive and Program

Syntax
RENAME <oldname> TO <newname>

Use
Renames the disk file specified by <oldname> to that specified by <newname>.

Examples
RENAME PEOPLE.DBF TO CLIENTS.DBF
Changes the name of the data file PEOPLE to CLIENTS.

RENAME B:ZIP.NDX TO B:ZIPCODE.NDX
Changes the name of the index file ZIP on drive B.

REPLACE

Application
Interactive and Program

Syntax
REPLACE <field(s)> WITH <value> [WHILE <condition>] [FOR <condition>]

Use
Changes the contents of a field or fields in selected records in the current data file.

Examples

REPLACE ALL PRICE WITH 100

Places the number 100 in the numeric field PRICE in all records in the data file.

REPLACE ALL STATE WITH "RI" FOR ZIP = "02906"

Places *RI* in the STATE field of all records which have the value 02906 in the ZIP field.

REPLACE QUANTITY WITH 12

Inserts the number 12 into the numeric field QUANTITY in the current record only.

REPORT FORM

Application

Interactive and Program

Syntax

REPORT FORM <report name> [WHILE <condition>] [FOR <condition>] [TO PRINT]

Use

Activates a report format previously created with the CREATE REPORT or MODIFY REPORT commands. See chapter 8 for more information on creating report files.

Examples

USE PEOPLE
REPORT FORM MAILING

Activates a report format named MAILING.FRM, and displays the resulting report onscreen.

USE STOCK INDEX ITEM_NO
REPORT FORM INVENTRY FOR VENDOR = "ACME" TO PRINT

Activates the report-format file INVENTRY.FRM and sends output to the printer. The report will include only records in which the field VENDOR contains *ACME.* Since an index is active, the records will appear in the order established by the index file ITEM_NO.

RESTORE

Application

Interactive and Program

Syntax

RESTORE FROM <filename> [ADDITIVE]

Use

Loads a set of memory variables from a memory variable file previously saved with the SAVE command. If the ADDITIVE option is not specified, the retrieved memory variables will replace all the variables currently in memory. To keep all current variables active, add the ADDITIVE clause to the command.

Examples

RESTORE FROM MEMFILE1

Loads the contents of MEMFILE1.MEM into memory. The loaded variables will replace any existing variables.

RESTORE FROM MEMFILE1 ADDITIVE

Loads the contents of MEMFILE1.MEM into memory. All existing variables will remain intact.

RUN/!

Application

Interactive and Program

Syntax

RUN <command>
! <command>

Use

Executes any valid DOS command as though it were typed directly at a DOS prompt. To use the RUN command (or the equivalent !), your computer must be equipped with more than 256K for DOS version 2.0 and higher, and more than 320K for DOS 3.0 and higher.

Caution: Do not use RUN or ! to activate a memory-resident program such as PRINT.COM or *Sidekick.* Instead, load these programs from DOS before entering *dBase III Plus.*

Examples

RUN WS

Runs a program called WS.COM (or WS.EXE or WS.BAT). Upon exiting this program, control returns to *dBase III Plus.*

RUN COMMAND

Activates the DOS command interpreter and places you into an auxiliary DOS mode. The computer will behave as though you were actually in DOS until you type EXIT, which returns control to *dBase III Plus.* This technique is handy if you have a number of DOS operations to perform at one time.

SAVE

Application

Interactive and Program

Syntax

SAVE TO <filename> [ALL LIKE/EXCEPT <skeleton>]

Use

Saves the contents of memory variables to a memory-variable (.MEM) file on disk for later use. You can use the asterisk and question mark in the skeleton; they have the same meaning as in DOS: A question mark represents a single unknown character, while the asterisk represents any number of unknown characters.

Examples

SAVE TO MEMS

Saves all currently defined memory variables to a file named MEMS.MEM.

SAVE TO SYS_STAT ALL LIKE SYS_*

Saves all memory variables with names beginning with the characters *SYS_* to a file named SYS_STAT.MEM.

SEEK

Application

Interactive and Program

Syntax

SEEK <expression>

Use

Searches for the first record in a data file which matches the specified <expression>. The file must be indexed, and <expression> must be of the same data type as the index key. SEEK is similar to FIND, except that FIND works with literal values and does not respond to expressions in quotes.

Examples

USE PEOPLE INDEX LASTNAME
SEEK "Smith"
Record = 43

USE LOANERS INDEX DUE_DATE
SEEK DATE( )
Record = 12

Finds the first record in which the index key (in this case the contents of a date field) matches the expression DATE( ), which is the current system date.

SELECT

Application

Interactive and Program

Syntax

SELECT <work area number 1–10 or letter *A–J* / alias>

Use

Allows relational and multifile operations by switching between the ten available work areas allowed by *dBase III Plus.* Each work area can have a different active data file, along with its associated format file and index files. By selecting a work area, either by name or number, or by the alias of the file currently in use in that work area, it becomes the active data file. Record selection and record-pointer movement commands affect only the active data file unless a file relation exists. (See the discussion of relational operations in chapter 7 for more detail.) Although up to ten data files can be in use at once, the total number of open files (database, index, and format) can not exceed 15.

Examples

SELECT 1
USE PEOPLE
DISPLAY

Record#	LNAME	FNAME	STREET	STATE ZIP
1	Finlay	Connie	127 Vincent Ave.	RI 02903

SELECT PEOPLE
DISPLAY

Record#	LNAME	FNAME	STREET	STATE ZIP
1	Finlay	Connie	127 Vincent Ave.	RI 02903

SELECT 2
USE STOCK
DISPLAY

Record#	ITEM_NO	TYPE	DESCRIP	COST
1	H4201	HAMMER	BALLPEEN	3.79

SET

Application

Interactive and Program

Syntax

SET

Use

Enters a menu-controlled mode in which the various environmental (SET) commands can be examined and changed. Each of the SET commands contained within the menu can also be changed directly from the dot prompt.

SET BELL

Application
Interactive and Program

Syntax
SET BELL ON/OFF

Default
ON

Use
Defines whether *dBase III Plus* should sound a bell when a field becomes filled or when an invalid entry is typed. For sanity's sake, set BELL to OFF.

SET COLOR

Application
Interactive and Program

Syntax
SET COLOR TO <front/back>,<front/back>,<border>

Default
White on Black, Black on White, Black

Use
Changes the screen colors on color monitors or the screen intensity on monochrome monitors.

Examples

SET COLOR TO W/B, R/W, B

For color monitors, this specifies white characters on a blue background for normal text, and red characters on a white background for enhanced areas (such as GETs). The border around the screen is set to blue. This is a nice combination for most applications.

SET COLOR TO W/N, W+/NU

For monochrome monitors, this specifies dim white characters on a black background for normal text, and bright white characters on underlines for enhanced areas. Border color does not apply to monochrome monitors.

SET CONFIRM

Application

Interactive and Program

Syntax

SET CONFIRM ON/OFF

Default

OFF

Use

Determines whether you must press Enter after typing data into field entries for full-screen operations such as APPEND or EDIT. With CONFIRM OFF, the cursor moves to the next field automatically when the field is filled. With CONFIRM ON, Enter must be pressed even when the field is filled.

SET CONSOLE

Application

Interactive and Program

Syntax

SET CONSOLE ON/OFF

Default

ON

Use

Suppresses display to the screen when OFF. This command is usually used to suppress the display of reports onscreen while they are being sent to the printer. Be careful with this command; when CONSOLE is OFF you cannot see keyboard input even though it still affects the system.

SET DECIMALS

Application

Interactive and Program

Syntax

SET DECIMALS TO <n>

Default

At least 2

Use

Determines how many decimal places are normally displayed with numeric values.

SET DEFAULT TO

Application

Interactive and Program

Syntax

SET DEFAULT TO <drive>

Default

The drive from which *dBase III Plus* was started

Use

Defines the default disk drive used for file storage.

Example

SET DEFAULT TO A:

SET DELETED

Application

Interactive and Program

Syntax

SET DELETED ON/OFF

Default

OFF

Use

Determines whether records marked for deletion are included in *dBase III Plus* commands. If DELETED is ON, the marked records are ignored by most commands.

SET DEVICE

Application

Interactive and Program

Syntax

SET DEVICE TO PRINT/SCREEN

Default

Screen

Use

Directs the display of SAY command to either the printer or the video screen. When DEVICE is set to PRINT, GET commands are ignored.

SET EXACT

Application

Interactive and Program

Syntax

SET EXACT ON/OFF

Default

OFF

Use

Determines whether a partial match will be accepted when performing string-based comparisons or searches.

Example

LOCATE FOR LASTNAME = "SMI"

With EXACT set to OFF, the following command can be used to find the last name *SMITH* in the LASTNAME field of a data file. With EXACT set to ON, the entire string (in this case *SMITH*) would have to be spelled out completely, since partial matches are ignored.

SET FIELDS

Application

Interactive and Program

Syntax

SET FIELDS ON/OFF
SET FIELDS TO <field list>

Default

OFF

Use

SET FIELDS TO <field list> specifies a group of fields within the current data file which are to be used in subsequent operations. SET FIELDS ON/OFF activates or deactivates the field list specified in the SET FIELDS TO command. With FIELDS set OFF, all of the fields in the current file are included in LIST, EDIT, or DISPLAY operations.

Example

SET FIELDS TO PART_NO, PRICE, ON_HAND

Establishes and activates a field list consisting of the fields PART_NO, PRICE, and ON_HAND. Only these fields can subsequently be displayed or changed.

SET FILTER TO

Application

Interactive and Program

Syntax

SET FILTER TO <condition>

Default

Inactive

Use

Causes the data file to appear as though it contains only those records which meet the specified condition. If no condition is specified, SET FILTER TO deactivates any active filters.

Examples

SET FILTER TO DUE_DATE <= DATE( )

Only those records in which the field DUE_DATE is the current date or earlier will appear.

SET FILTER TO

Cancels any active filters.

SET FORMAT TO

Application

Interactive and Program

Syntax

SET FORMAT TO <.FMT filename>

Default

Inactive

Use

Activates a screen-format file which controls the screen layout during EDIT and APPEND operations. If no format is active, all active fields are used and appear in the upper left-hand corner of the screen.

Examples

SET FORMAT TO ITEMS

Activates a format file named ITEMS.FMT which controls screen format during subsequent full-screen operations.

SET FORMAT TO

Deactivates an active format file. A format file will also be closed when the CLOSE FORMAT, CLOSE DATABASE, or USE commands are executed.

SET FUNCTION

Application

Interactive and Program

Syntax

SET FUNCTION <2–10> TO <expression>

Defaults

F1 HELP
F2 ASSIST
F3 LIST
F4 DIR
F5 DISPLAY STRUCTURE
F6 DISPLAY STATUS
F7 DISPLAY MEMORY
F8 DISPLAY
F9 APPEND
F10 EDIT

Use

Allows you to redefine the string assigned to one of the computer's function keys. This command is used with often-typed commands to increase productivity. Function key F1 is always dedicated to HELP, and cannot be programmed.

Examples

SET FUNCTION 5 TO "CLEAR;"

Assigns the command CLEAR to function key F5. The semicolon after the command causes an Enter to take place as well, as though the command were typed from the keyboard.

SET FUNCTION 7 TO "USE PARTS; LIST NEXT 10;"

Programs the function key F7 so that it enters USE PARTS and then enters LIST NEXT 10.

SET HELP

Application

Interactive and Program

Syntax

SET HELP ON/OFF

Default

ON

Use

Determines whether *dBase III Plus* offers help automatically whenever a command is entered incorrectly. When the offer *Do you want some help?* is made, responding with a *Y* will display a help screen for the command you entered incorrectly.

SET INDEX TO

Application

Interactive and Program

Syntax

SET INDEX TO <filename.NDX list>

Default

None

Use

Activates one or more index files for the current data file. The first file specified in a list of several files is the master index and controls the order of the data file. Up to seven index files may be open for a given data file.

Examples

USE PEOPLE
SET INDEX TO LASTNAME, STATE

Opens the index files LASTNAME.NDX and STATE.NDX, and assigns LASTNAME as the master index.

SET INDEX TO

Closes all open index files.

SET MARGIN

Application

Interactive and Program

Syntax

SET MARGIN TO <n>

Default

0

Use

Sets the left margin for all output sent to the printer.

Example

SET MARGIN TO 8

Establishes a left margin of eight character spaces on all printed output.

SET MEMOWIDTH

Application

Interactive and Program

Syntax

SET MEMOWIDTH TO <n>

Default

50

Use

Sets the width of data displayed from memo fields. The minimum value for this command is 8, and the maximum is established by the printer or screen width.

SET ORDER TO

Application

Interactive and Program

Syntax

SET ORDER TO <n>

Default

1

Use

Selects which of the active index files will control record order. The numbers 1–7 are assigned consecutively to the index files opened with the SET INDEX TO command. The corresponding numbers identify the indices to this command.

Examples:

USE MEMBERS INDEX MEM_NO,LASTNAME,ZIP
SET ORDER TO 2

Establishes LASTNAME.NDX as the master index file controlling record order. All other indices remain active.

SET ORDER TO 0

Disables index control of record order, but keeps all active index files updated with changes made to the data file. With ORDER set to 0, records appear in record-number order.

SET PATH

Application

Interactive and Program

Syntax

SET PATH TO <pathname>

Default

Current DOS directory

Use

Instructs *dBase III Plus* where to look for files if they are not found in the current (default) drive and directory.

Examples

SET PATH TO \DBASE\PROJECT1

If a file is not found in the current directory, *dBase III Plus* will look for it in \DBASE\PROJECT1.

SET PATH TO B:

Causes *dBase III Plus* to look in the root directory of drive B for files not found in the current directory.

SET PRINT

Application

Interactive and Program

Syntax

SET PRINT ON/OFF

Default

OFF

Use

Specifies whether output will be routed to the printer in addition to the screen. Information displayed with @...SAY or @...GET commands is not affected; these commands are routed according to the SET DEVICE command.

SET PRINTER

Application

Interactive and Program

Syntax

SET PRINTER TO <device>

Default

LPT1

Use

Directs printer output to a selected device. Often used to direct output to the desired device when multiple printers are available.

Examples

SET PRINTER TO LPT2

Directs printer output to the computer's second parallel port, LPT2.

SET PRINTER TO COM1

Redirects printer output to the first serial port.

SET RELATION

Application

Interactive and Program

Syntax

SET RELATION TO <key> INTO <filename>

Default

Inactive

Use

Establishes relations between two open data files. The files must be opened in separate work areas, and the file into which the relation is being set must have an active index based on the specified key.

Example

SELECT 1
USE INVOICES
SELECT 2
USE ITEMS INDEX INV_NO
SELECT 1
SET RELATION TO INV_NO INTO ITEMS

This establishes a relation between the file in work area 1 (INVOICES) and the file in work area 2 (ITEMS). Whenever the record pointer in work area 1 is moved, the record pointer in work area 2 will be repositioned to a matching record as well.

SET SAFETY

Application

Interactive and Program

Syntax

SET SAFETY ON/OFF

Default

ON

Use

Determines whether *dBase III Plus* will display a warning message prior to executing commands which will overwrite or destroy an existing file.

Example

SET SAFETY ON
USE NAMES
INDEX ON LASTNAME TO LAST
LAST.NDX already exists, overwrite it? (Y/N)

SET STATUS

Application

Interactive and Program

Syntax

SET STATUS ON/OFF

Default

ON

Use

Activates or deactivates the status display bar at the bottom of the screen.

SET TALK

Application

Interactive and Program

Syntax

SET TALK ON/OFF

Default

ON

Use

Determines whether the result of commands such as COUNT, SUM, or AVERAGE is displayed on the screen. Normally, TALK is set ON during interactive (dot-prompt) operations and is set OFF during program execution.

SKIP

Application

Interactive and Program

Syntax

SKIP [<n>]

Use

Moves the record pointer one or more positions within the file. If a negative number is used for <n>, the pointer is moved backwards.

Example

? RECNO( )
15
SKIP
? RECNO( )
16
SKIP 4
? RECNO( )
20
SKIP −9
? RECNO( )
11

SORT

Application

Interactive and Program

Syntax

SORT ON <field> TO <filename>

Use

Creates a new data file from records in the current file, arranged according to the contents of the specified <field>. SORT does not affect the contents of the original file. In most cases, it is more efficient to index a file rather than to sort it.

Examples

USE PEOPLE
SORT ON LASTNAME TO PEOPLE2

Creates a new file called PEOPLE2.DBF, which contains the records found in the current database arranged in ascending alphabetical order according to the contents of the LASTNAME field.

SORT ON LASTNAME/D TO PEOPLE2
The same as above, but arranges the new file in descending rather than ascending order.

USE ITEMS
SORT ON PART_NO TO PARTS FIELDS PART_NO, PRICE
Creates a new file called PARTS.DBF containing only the fields PART_NO and PRICE from the records in ITEMS.DBF, arranged by PART_NO.

SUM

Application

Interactive and Program

Syntax

SUM <fieldname> [TO <memory variable>] [WHILE <condition>] [FOR <condition>]

Use

Adds the values found in the specified numeric field for all records or for those records meeting the optional condition.

Examples

USE ITEMS
SUM QUANT FOR VENDOR = "ACME"
125 records summed
QUANT
4375
Shows that the total of the values in the QUANT field for all records in which the VENDOR field contains *ACME* is 4375.

USE MEMBERS
SUM GIFT TO TOTAL_GIFT
15 records summed
GIFT
15000
? TOTAL_GIFT
15000

Adds the values found in the numeric field GIFT in all records. Also stores the result in the memory variable named TOTAL_GIFT.

USE

Application

Interactive and Program

Syntax

USE <filename> [INDEX <filename>] [ALIAS <name>]

Use

Opens a data file and up to seven associated index files. A file must be in use before performing any operations on it.

Examples

USE PEOPLE

Opens the data file PEOPLE.DBF.

USE PARTS INDEX PART_NO, LOCATION

Opens the data file PARTS.DBF and the index files PART_NO and LOCATION. Since PART_NO was listed first, it controls record order.

USE PARTS ALIAS ITEMS

Opens the data file PARTS and assigns it the alias name ITEMS. Subsequent operations can refer to the file as either PARTS or ITEMS.

ZAP

Application

Interactive and Program

Syntax

ZAP

Use

Deletes all records from the active data file. Use with extreme care. The prompt, *ZAP <filename>? (Y/N),* is displayed only if SAFETY is set ON; otherwise the command is executed immediately.

Example

USE PEOPLE
ZAP
ZAP PEOPLE.DBF? (Y/N)

If answered with a *Y,* all of the records in PEOPLE.DBF will be deleted.

Chapter 6

dBase III Plus Functions

Chapter 6

dBase III Plus Functions

dBase has a library of built-in functions which greatly extend the program's power and flexibility. Functions are available for character-string manipulation, arithmetic operations, date and time operations, and data-file control. Proper use of functions can make it possible to perform many tasks which would be difficult, if not impossible, otherwise.

Functions can be identified by a pair of parentheses which enclose a value called the *argument.* Every function processes this value in some way and returns a *result.* The value can be the contents of a data field, a memory variable, a number, a literal string of characters, or even the result returned by another function. The kind of data returned by the function is specific to the function.

The UPPER( ) function is typical. It returns the uppercase equivalent of the character string or field enclosed within the parentheses:

DISPLAY NAME
John Smith

DISPLAY UPPER(NAME)
JOHN SMITH

? UPPER("here is another string")
HERE IS ANOTHER STRING

Other string functions are used to dissect a character string by returning a specified portion of the argument:

? LEFT("Bob Smith",5)
Bob S

Numeric functions process numbers in much the same way. For example, SQRT( ) returns the square root of the argument:

? SQRT(900)
30

Functions also make it possible to perform operations on two different types of data by converting information from one type to another. The VAL( ) function is an example. It returns a numeric value from a character string that is made of numeric characters:

? VAL("4")
4

Conversion functions are especially important when working with dates. Since dates cannot be entered directly from the keyboard, using a character-to-date conversion function on a character string allows you to achieve the same result:

LOCATE FOR DUE_DATE = CTOD("12/15/86")

Likewise, the DTOC( ) function converts date information into character strings:

? "The due date is " + DTOC(DUE_DATE)
The due date is 01/07/87

Some functions are used in tests, to determine whether something is true or false, or to determine some aspect of system operation. The FOUND( ) function returns a logical TRUE if the result of the preceding LOCATE, FIND, or SEEK was successful. Otherwise, FOUND( ) returns logical FALSE:

LOCATE FOR PART_NO = "J4450-A"
? FOUND( )
.T.

This indicates that the LOCATE was successful; a record was found matching the comparison.

Notice that FOUND( ) has no argument within the parentheses. A number of *dBase III* plus functions require no argument, although they still return a result of their action. The DATE( ) and TIME( ) functions are further examples of this type of function. Each needs no argument, yet returns the requested value (in this case, the current system date and time).

Nesting functions allows a value to be processed in several different ways with one operation. For example, combine the UPPER( ) and SUBSTR( ) functions to return the uppercase equivalent of a portion of a character string:

? UPPER(SUBSTR("Massachusetts",3,4))
SSAC

This combination of functions takes four characters of the string, beginning at the third character, and turns them into uppercase. The UPPER( ) function acts on the value returned by the action of the SUBSTR( ) function contained within it.

The following is a list of functions that are most useful to the *dBase III Plus* user. For information on some of the more advanced functions, consult the *dBase III Plus* user's manual.

The following conventions are used in the function descriptions:

Symbol	**Definition**
< >	Indicates information which must be supplied by the user. The brackets themselves are not to be entered.
[ ]	Indicates information which is optional in the use of the function.
/	Indicates that the function can be used in more than one way. Enter only one of the options found on either side of the slash.
<n>	A numeric expression.
<c>	A character expression.
<d>	A date.
<condition>	A user-specified condition.

ABS( )

Syntax

ABS(<n>)

Use

Returns the absolute value of the argument. In effect, the function makes all numbers positive, regardless of whether they were positive or negative to begin with.

Example

? ABS(−12)
12

ASC( )

Syntax

ASC(<c>)

Use

Returns the ASCII value of a single character or of the leftmost character in a string used as the argument. The value returned is between 0 and 255, and corresponds to the argument's position within the IBM extended character set.

Examples

? ASC("+")
43

? ASC("APPLE")
65

AT( )

Syntax

AT(<c1>,<c2>)

Use

Returns a number corresponding to the starting position of string <c1> within string <c2>. If the first string is not contained within the second, the function returns the value 0. The AT( ) function is an alternative to the $ (is-contained-within) operator. By testing to see if the value returned by AT( ) is greater than zero, you can determine whether one string is part of another.

Examples

? AT('pool','swimming pool and tennis court')
10

STORE "Bob J. Anderson" TO NAME
? AT('Robert',NAME)
0

BOF( )

Syntax

BOF( )

Use

Indicates whether the record pointer is at the beginning of a file. No argument is required. A logical true (.T.) is returned if the record pointer is positioned before the first record in the data file, and logical false (.F.) is returned if it is not. This function is often used to see whether the record pointer is at the beginning of a file when moving the record pointer backward with SKIP. BOF( ) has the opposite effect of EOF( ), which tests whether the end of a file has been reached.

Example

USE PEOPLE
? RECNO( )
1
? BOF( )
.F.
SKIP −1
? BOF( )
.T.

CDOW( )

Syntax

CDOW(<d>)

Use

Returns a character-string representation of the day of the week for the date in the date expression. Each day is spelled out completely, with the first character capitalized.

Example

? DATE( )
03/29/87
? CDOW(DATE( ))
Sunday

CHR( )

Syntax

CHR(<n>)

Use

Returns the ASCII character with the code value of <n>, which must be an integer between 0 and 255. A common use of the CHR( ) function is to send special control codes to a printer. This function is the opposite of ASC( ).

Examples

? CHR(69)
E

? CHR(7)
[The computer will sound a short beep.]

CMONTH( )

Syntax

CMONTH(<d>)

Use

Returns a character-string representing the month in the date expression. The month names are spelled out completely, with the first letter capitalized.

Example

? DATE( )
03/29/87
? CMONTH(DATE( ))
March

COL( )

Syntax

COL( )

Use

Returns an integer between 0 and 79, corresponding to the current column number of the screen cursor. No argument is required. This function is often used to position information on screen a certain number of spaces from the current cursor position. Programmers use the COL( ) function to test whether information is being placed in the proper screen position.

Example

@ 10, 1 SAY "This is some text"
@ 10, COL( )+10 SAY "This text is ten spaces further right."

CTOD( )

Syntax

CTOD(<c>)

Use

Performs a character-to-date conversion. The string used as <c> must be in a format that corresponds to the current setting of the SET DATE command (normally MM/DD/YY or MM/DD/YYYY). Since dates cannot be entered directly from the keyboard, the CTOD( ) function makes it possible to perform comparisons based on date fields. The reverse of the CTOD( ) function is DTOC( ), which performs a date-to-character conversion.

Examples

LOCATE FOR DUE_DATE = CTOD("01/01/86")

REPLACE ALL EXP_DATE WITH CTOD("09/30/87")

DATE( )

Syntax

DATE( )

Use

Returns the current system date as set by the computer's operating system. No argument is required. The value returned is a valid date expression in the form MM/DD/YY (or MM/DD/YYYY if CENTURY is set ON). The accuracy of this date depends on the accuracy of the date in your computer's operating system. If the computer does not have a built-in clock/calendar, the date must be typed in when the computer is started.

Examples

LOCATE FOR DUE_DATE <= DATE( )

? "Today is "+CTOD(DATE( ))
Today is 06/01/87

DAY( )

Syntax

DAY(<d>)

Use

Returns an integer value corresponding to the day of the month for the date in the date expression.

Example

? DATE( )
03/29/87
? DAY(DATE( ))
29

DBF( )

Syntax

DBF( )

Use

Returns the name of the database file currently in use. No argument is required. If no file is open, nothing is returned.

Examples

USE PEOPLE
? DBF( )
C:PEOPLE.DBF

USE
? DBF( )

DELETED( )

Syntax

DELETED( )

Use

Indicates whether a record is marked for deletion. No argument is required. A logical true (.T.) is returned for records within the data file which are marked for deletion, and a logical false (.F.) for unmarked records. This function can be used to find, count, or list records that are marked for deletion, or to test whether a single record is marked.

Examples

COUNT FOR DELETED( )
15 Records

LOCATE FOR DELETED( )
Record = 35

? DELETED( )
.F.

DISKSPACE( )

Syntax

DISKSPACE( )

Use

Returns the number of bytes available on the current disk drive. No argument is required. This function is often used to check whether enough space is available before performing a disk-intensive operation such as SORT or COPY.

Example

? DISKSPACE( )
186000

DOW( )

Syntax

DOW(<d>)

Use

Returns an integer value between 1 and 7, corresponding to the day of the week for the date in the expression <d>. A value of 1 represents Sunday; 7 is Saturday.

Example

? DATE( )
03/29/87
? CDOW(DATE( ))
Sunday
? DOW(DATE( ))
1

DTOC( )

Syntax

DTOC(<d>)

Use

Performs a date-to-character conversion on the date expression. This function makes it possible to combine date values with character strings. The string value returned is in the form MM/DD/YY unless SET DATE or SET CENTURY are changed, in which case the format follows that specified in the SET DATE command. This function has the opposite effect of CTOD( ).

Example

? "Today is "+DTOC(DATE( ))
Today is 09/30/87

EOF( )

Syntax

EOF( )

Use

Indicates whether the record pointer is at the end of a file. No argument is required. A logical true (.T.) is returned if the record pointer is at the end of a file, and a logical false (.F.), if it is not. This function is often used to test whether a search (LOCATE, FIND, SEEK) was successful; when EOF( ) returns .T., the operation was unsuccessful.

Examples

LOCATE FOR NAME = "Bob Jones"
? EOF( )
.F.
[Indicates that the record was found.]

SKIP
? EOF( )
.F.
SKIP
? EOF( )
.T.
[Indicates that the second SKIP brought the record pointer past the last record in the file.]

EXP( )

Syntax

EXP(<n>)

Use

Returns the result of the exponential function of e<^{n}>. The value passed to the expression is used as the exponent. This function is the opposite of the LOG( ) function.

Examples

? EXP(5)
148.41

? EXP(1)
2.72

FIELD( )

Syntax

FIELD(<n>)

Use

Returns the name of the field in the current data file whose field number within the file structure is <n>.

Example

USE PEOPLE
? FIELD(1)
LASTNAME
? FIELD(3)
ADDRESS

FILE( )

Syntax

FILE ("<filename.extension>")

Use

Returns a logical value indicating whether a file with the specified name exists on the default disk, or on a specified disk. The complete filename, including extension, must be specified.

Examples

? FILE("PEOPLE.DBF")
.T.
[Shows that the data file PEOPLE exists on the default disk.]

? FILE("A:MONTHLY.NDX")
.F.
[Shows that there is no index file named MONTHLY on the disk in drive A.]

FOUND( )

Syntax

FOUND( )

Use

Returns a logical true (.T.) if the result of the previous LOCATE, CONTINUE, SEEK, or FIND was successful. No argument is required. After a successful find, any movement of the record pointer other than with these commands sets FOUND( ) to .F.

Examples

LOCATE FOR NAME = "Dave Carrol"
? FOUND( )
.T.
[Shows that a record was found that matches the search criterion.]

SEEK "XY-47"
? FOUND( )
.F.
[Indicates that no record was found to match the search criterion.]

IIF( )

Syntax

IIF(<test>,<if_pass>,<if_fail>)

Use

Evaluates the logical expression <test> to determine whether it is true or false. If the test is true, the function returns the value contained in <if_pass>. If the expression evaluates to .F., the value in <if_fail> is returned. Both expressions (<if_pass> and <if_fail>) must be of the same data type.

The Immediate If function can be used in a mailing-label format or in a report. For example, you could use the function in the contents of a report field to translate a logical field into a more informative form.

Example

TAX = IIF(STATE="CA",.05,0)
[Sets the value for sales tax to .05 if STATE equals *CA*, and to 0 otherwise.]

REPLACE ALL SALUTATION WITH IIF(GENDER="M","Mr.","Ms.")
[Replaces the contents of the SALUTATION field with *Mr.* for those records which contain *M* in the GENDER field, and puts *Ms.* into SALUTATION in all other records.]

IIF(IS_MEMBER,"Member","Nonmember")
[This will return *Member* if the logical field IS_MEMBER contains a true, and will return *Nonmember* otherwise.]

INT( )

Syntax

INT(<n>)

Use

Returns the integer value of numeric expression <n>. Any digits to the right of the decimal point are removed, and only those to the left of the decimal point are returned. The number is not rounded; the fractional portion is simply truncated. Use the ROUND( ) function to round a number to the nearest whole integer value.

Examples

? INT(10.5)
10

? INT(237.993)
237

ISALPHA( )

Syntax

ISALPHA(<c>)

Use

Returns a logical true (.T.) if the first character of the string <c> is an upper- or lowercase alphabetic character between *A* and *Z*. A logical false (.F.) is returned otherwise.

Examples

? ISALPHA("Hello")
.T.

? ISALPHA("123 Main Street")
.F.

? ISALPHA("Phone 555-2354")
.T.

ISCOLOR( )

Syntax

ISCOLOR( )

Use

Indicates whether the computer is equipped with color/graphics adapter hardware. No argument is required. The function returns a logical true (.T.) if the hardware is present, meaning that colors can be used in the display. A logical false (.F) is returned otherwise. This function is primarily used by programmers to determine whether a program is being used on a monochrome or color system.

ISLOWER( )

Syntax

ISLOWER(<c>)

Use

Returns a logical true (.T.) if the first character of the string <c> is a lowercase character between *a* and *z*. If the first character is uppercase or nonalphabetic, a logical false (.F.) is returned.

Examples

? ISLOWER("hello")
.T.

? ISLOWER("Hello")
.F.

? ISLOWER("123 Main Street")
.F.

ISUPPER( )

Syntax

ISUPPER(<c>)

Use

Returns a logical true (.T.) if the first character of the string <c> is an uppercase character between *A* and *Z.* If the first character is lowercase or nonalphabetic, a logical false (.F.) is returned.

Examples

? ISUPPER("hello")
.F.

? ISUPPER("Hello")
.T.

? ISUPPER("123 Main Street")
.F.

LEFT( )

Syntax

LEFT(<c>,<n>)

Use

LEFT( ) returns the leftmost characters of character string <c>, beginning at the first character and extending <n> characters into the string. If <n> is larger than the number of characters in the string, the entire string is returned.

Examples

? LEFT("This is a string",7)
This is

? LEFT("ABCDE",1)
A

? LEFT("HELLO",10)
HELLO

LEN( )

Syntax

LEN(<c>)

Use

Returns the number of characters in the string <c>. When using the function to determine the length of information in a data field, it's important to remember that LEN( ) always returns the specified length of the field, regardless of the field's contents. For example, using LEN( ) on a field 35 characters wide will always return 35, even if the field actually contains fewer characters or is completely empty. To determine the actual length of the contents of a character field, use the TRIM( ) function in conjunction with LEN( ).

Examples

? LEN("Welcome Home")
12

? NAME
Bob Jones
? LEN(NAME)
35
? LEN(TRIM(NAME))
9

LOG( )

Syntax

LOG(<n>)

Use

Returns the natural logarithm of the numeric expression <n>. The natural logarithm is the logarithm to the base *e* (2.71828). This function is the opposite of EXP( ).

Examples

? LOG(2.71828)
1

? LOG(10)
2.30

LOWER( )

Syntax

LOWER(<c>)

Use

Returns a string equivalent to the argument string <c>, but with all uppercase alphabetic characters converted to lowercase. The function has no effect on characters which are not uppercase alphabetics.

Examples

? LOWER("Hello")
hello

? LOWER("THE PRICE IS $6.95")
the price is $6.95

LTRIM( )

Syntax

LTRIM(<c>)

Use

Removes any leading blanks from a character expression. This function is similar to TRIM( ), but it affects the left side of the character expression instead of the right. It is most often used to process strings which were created from numeric expressions with the STR( ) function.

Examples

? NAME
Bob Jones
? LTRIM(NAME)
Bob Jones

? STR(123,5)
  123
? LTRIM(STR(123,5))
123

MAX( )

Syntax

MAX(<n1>,<n2>)

Use

Returns the greater of the two numeric values <n1> and <n2>.

Examples

? MAX(10,20)
20

? MAX(2+2,9/3)
4

MIN( )

Syntax

MIN(<n1>,<n2>)

Use

Returns the smaller of the two numeric values <n1> and <n2>.

Examples

? MIN(10,20)
10

? MIN(2+2,9/3)
3

MOD( )

Syntax

MOD(<n1>,<n2>)

Use

Returns the modulus (remainder) of <n1> divided by <n2>. This function is often used in conversion formulas, such as inches to yards, or minutes to hours.

Examples

? MOD(100/7)
2
[100/7 yields 14 with a remainder of 2]

To convert 7000 feet to miles:
? INT(7000/5280)
1
[Number of whole miles]

? MOD(7000/5280)
1720
[Number of feet remaining]

MONTH( )

Syntax

MONTH(<d>)

Use

Returns a number between 1 and 12 representing the month of the year expressed in the date <d>.

Examples

? MONTH(DATE( ))
4

? MONTH(CTOD("11/10/88"))
11

NDX( )

Syntax

NDX(<n>)

Use

Returns the name of an active index file for the current data file. The number <n> corresponds to the number of the index file, and must be between 1 and 7. The number of a particular index file is determined by the order in which the index files were opened. If no index file with the specified number is active, nothing is returned.

Examples

USE PEOPLE INDEX NAME,ZIP
? NDX(2)
ZIP.NDX

USE PEOPLE (no index specified)
? NDX(1)
[A null string is returned.]

OS( )

Syntax

OS( )

Use

Returns the name and version number of the operating system currently in use on the computer. No argument is required.

Example

? OS( )
MS-DOS 2.11

PCOL( )

Syntax

PCOL( )

Use

Returns a number corresponding to the current column (horizontal) position of the printer's printhead. No argument is required. The function is used primarily by programmers to track the position at which characters will be displayed in printer output.

Example

SET DEVICE TO PRINT
? "HELLO"
SET DEVICE TO SCREEN
? PCOL( )
6

PROW( )

Syntax

PROW( )

Use

Returns a number corresponding to the current row (vertical) position of the printer's printhead. No argument is required. Usually used by programmers to determine when one page is full and a new page is needed.

Example

SET DEVICE TO PRINT
? "HELLO"
SET DEVICE TO SCREEN
? PROW()
3

RECCOUNT( )

Syntax

RECCOUNT( )

Use

Returns the number of records in the active data file. No argument is required. All records, including those marked for deletion, are included in the count.

Example

USE PEOPLE
? RECCOUNT()
75
[Indicates that there are 75 records in the file PEOPLE.]

RECNO( )

Syntax

RECNO( )

Use

Returns the current position of the record pointer. No argument is required. The value returned will be one larger than the highest record number if the end-of-file, EOF( ), condition is true.

Example

USE PEOPLE
GO 4
? RECNO( )
4
SKIP
? RECNO( )
5
SKIP −2
? RECNO( )
3

RECSIZE( )

Syntax

RECSIZE( )

Use

Returns the number of bytes occupied by each record in the current data file. No argument is required. This function is useful for determining how many records will fit on a disk for purposes of copying and backups.

However, simply multiplying the value returned by RECSIZE( ) by the value returned by RECCOUNT( ) does not give an accurate picture of data-file size since it does not include the size of the file header. To determine the actual size of a data file, first calculate the header size with the formula:

Header Size = (32 * <number of fields>) + 32

Next, add this to the value calculated by multiplying RECCOUNT( ) by RECSIZE( ), and you will know the exact size of the data file.

Example

USE PEOPLE
? RECSIZE( )
75

REPLICATE( )

Syntax

REPLICATE(<c>,<n>)

Use

Returns a character string comprised of <n> occurrences of the string <c>. The string to be replicated can be more than one character long, but the resulting string generated by the function must be no more than 254 characters long. By specifying a CHR( ) value for <c>, it is possible to access the IBM's extended character set and use the special graphics characters in your applications.

Examples

? REPLICATE("#",10)
##########

REPLICATE(CHR(65),15)
AAAAAAAAAAAAAAA

? REPLICATE(CHR(205),80)
[Creates a double horizontal line across the width of the screen.]

RIGHT( )

Syntax

RIGHT(<c>,<n>)

Use

Returns the rightmost <n> characters from the string <c>. If <n> is greater than the length of <c>, the entire string is returned.

Examples

? RIGHT("This is a string",7)
string

? RIGHT("ABCDE",1)
E

? RIGHT("Hello",10)
Hello

ROUND( )

Syntax

ROUND(<n1>,<n2>)

Use

Rounds the number <n1> to the number of decimal places specified by <n2>.

Examples

? ROUND(3.1415926,4)
3.1416

? ROUND(123.7,0)
124

ROW( )

Syntax

ROW( )

Use

Returns a number between 0 and 24 indicating the current vertical position of the cursor on the screen. No argument is required. This function is primarily used by programmers to keep track of screen locations.

Examples

? ROW( )
10

@ROW( )−5,5 SAY "This is five rows above the last text displayed"

RTRIM( )

See TRIM( )

SPACE( )

Syntax

SPACE(<n>)

Use

Returns a series of <n> blank space characters.

Examples

? SPACE(10)+"Hello"
          Hello

? "This is separated"+SPACE(15)+"by fifteen spaces."
This is separated   by fifteen spaces.

SQRT( )

Syntax

SQRT(<n>)

Use

Returns the square root of numeric expression <n>. The decimal precision of the function is determined by the SET DECIMALS command.

Examples

? SQRT(9)
3.00

SET DECIMALS TO 4
? SQRT(7)
2.6458

STR( )

Syntax

STR(<n>[<length>][<decimal>])

Use

Returns a character string representing the value of the numeric variable <n>. Unless the length or number of decimal places is specified, a string with a length of 10 characters is returned and decimal places are truncated. You can specify the length of the string by adding a <length> value, and the number of decimal places by adding a <decimal> value. This function is the opposite of VAL( ).

Examples

? STR(1234.567)
1234

? STR(1234.567,8,3)
1234.567

STUFF( )

Syntax

STUFF(<c1>,<start>,<extent>,<c2>)

Use

Inserts character string <c2> into character string <c1>, optionally replacing a portion of the existing contents of <c1>. The numeric value <start> determines the position within string <c1> at which string <c2> will be inserted, and the numeric value <extent> specifies how many characters you want removed from string <c1> at the insertion point. Use a value of 0 for <extent> if you want <c2> inserted into <c1> without overwriting any of the existing contents of string <c1>. By specifying a null string (" ") for <c2>, the function can be used to remove characters from <c1>.

Examples

? STUFF("My name is Dave",12,4,"Bill")
My name is Bill

? STUFF("This is a test",9,0,"not ")
This is not a test

? STUFF("abcdefg",3,3," ")
abfg

SUBSTR( )

Syntax

SUBSTR(<c>,<start>[,<extent>])

Use

Returns a substring of the string <c> beginning at the character position specified by the numeric expression <start>. If a numeric value is specified for <extent>, then only that number of characters will be returned. If the <extent> value specifies more characters than are in the portion of the string beginning at position <start>, then only the existing number of characters will be returned.

Examples

? SUBSTR("This is a test",7)
s a test

? SUBSTR("This is a test",6,4)
is a

TIME( )

Syntax

TIME( )

Use

Returns the current time from the computer's operating system. No argument is required. The value is returned in a character string in military (24-hour) format.

Example

? TIME( )
13:45:09
[Indicates that the current system time is just after 1:45 p.m.]

TRANSFORM( )

Syntax

TRANSFORM(<c>/<n>,<format string>)

Use

Converts a numeric or character expression into a character expression with the format specified by <format string>. The result is similar to using the SAY command along with a PICTURE clause.

Examples

? NAME
Bob Jones
? TRANSFORM(NAME,"@! X X X X X X X X X X X")
B O B J O N E S

? TRANSFORM(1234000,"#,###,###.##")
1,234,000.00

TRIM( )

Syntax

TRIM(<c>)

Use

Removes any trailing blanks from character expression <c>. This function is often used to remove blanks from character-field data. TRIM( ) is identical to RTRIM( ). Use the LTRIM( ) function to remove any blanks preceding a character string.

Example

? NAME
Bob Jones
? LEN(NAME)
35
? LEN(TRIM(NAME))
9

TYPE( )

Syntax

TYPE(<c>)

Returns a one-character code indicating the field or memory variable type of character expression <c>. The code values returned are:

C character
N numeric
L logical
M memo
D date
U undefined

The code U, for undefined, is returned when no field or memory variable exists with the name specified in the expression <c>.

Examples

? TYPE(PRICE)
N

? TYPE(NAME)
C

? TYPE(RATING)
U

UPPER( )

Syntax

UPPER(<c>)

Use

Returns a string equivalent to the argument string <c>, but with all lowercase alphabetic characters converted to uppercase. The function has no effect on characters in the string which are not lowercase alphabetics. UPPER( ) is often used in FOR and WHILE clauses to eliminate unwanted character-case distinctions.

Examples

? UPPER("Hello there")
HELLO THERE

LOCATE FOR UPPER(NAME) = BOB SMITH
Record = 45

? UPPER("123 Main Street)
123 MAIN STREET

VAL( )

Syntax

VAL(<c>)

Use

Returns the numeric value represented by the numeric digit characters in the string <c>. If the string contains no characters representing numeric digits, the function returns the value 0. This function has the opposite effect of STR( ).

Examples

? VAL("123")
123

? VAL("XYZ")
0

VERSION( )

Syntax

VERSION( )

Use

Returns the version number of *dBase III Plus.* An added feature of the VERSION function—undocumented by Ashton-Tate—is its ability to identify the exact version number and release date of the copy of *dBase III Plus* you are using. This feature is activated by using the number 1 as an argument.

Examples

? VERSION( )
dBASE III PLUS VERSION 1.1

? VERSION(1)
dBASE III PLUS VERSION 2.0x100 (07/24/86)

YEAR( )

Syntax

YEAR(<d>)

Use

Returns a four-digit numeric value representing the year in the date expression <d>.

Examples

? YEAR(CTOD("12/13/85")
1985

? YEAR(DATE( ))
1987

Chapter 7
Putting Files in Order

Chapter 7

Putting Files in Order

One of the most important features of a database program is its ability to arrange—or sort—records within a file. You may need a list of names arranged alphabetically, or a file of inventory items sorted by cost, or perhaps a customer list arranged by date of last order. *dBase III Plus* provides a number of methods for changing record order, each with its own advantages and limitations.

Figure 7-1. Reorganizing a File

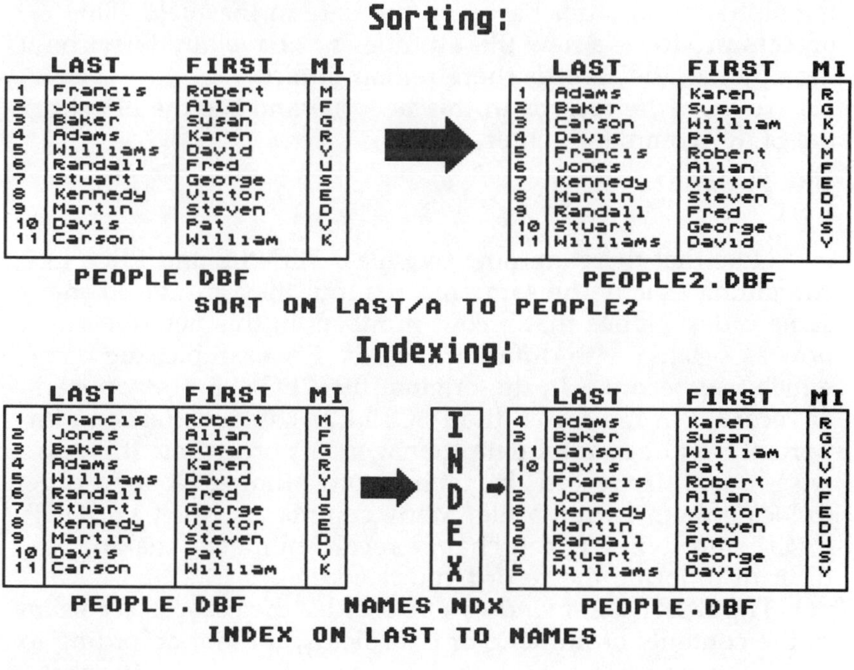

Sorting:

	LAST	FIRST	MI
1	Francis	Robert	M
2	Jones	Allan	F
3	Baker	Susan	G
4	Adams	Karen	R
5	Williams	David	Y
6	Randall	Fred	U
7	Stuart	George	S
8	Kennedy	Victor	E
9	Martin	Steven	D
10	Davis	Pat	V
11	Carson	William	K

PEOPLE.DBF

	LAST	FIRST	MI
1	Adams	Karen	R
2	Baker	Susan	G
3	Carson	William	K
4	Davis	Pat	V
5	Francis	Robert	M
6	Jones	Allan	F
7	Kennedy	Victor	E
8	Martin	Steven	D
9	Randall	Fred	U
10	Stuart	George	S
11	Williams	David	Y

PEOPLE2.DBF

SORT ON LAST/A TO PEOPLE2

Indexing:

	LAST	FIRST	MI
1	Francis	Robert	M
2	Jones	Allan	F
3	Baker	Susan	G
4	Adams	Karen	R
5	Williams	David	Y
6	Randall	Fred	U
7	Stuart	George	S
8	Kennedy	Victor	E
9	Martin	Steven	D
10	Davis	Pat	V
11	Carson	William	K

PEOPLE.DBF

INDEX

NAMES.NDX

	LAST	FIRST	MI
4	Adams	Karen	R
3	Baker	Susan	G
11	Carson	William	K
10	Davis	Pat	V
1	Francis	Robert	M
2	Jones	Allan	F
8	Kennedy	Victor	E
9	Martin	Steven	D
6	Randall	Fred	U
7	Stuart	George	S
5	Williams	David	Y

PEOPLE.DBF

INDEX ON LAST TO NAMES

Sorting

The most straightforward method of changing record order is to sort the file. When the SORT command is used, *dBase* creates a new file containing the records found in the file currently in use, but rearranged in a specified order. The SORT command needs to be given three pieces of information: the field on which you want the file sorted, the order in which you want the file sorted (ascending or descending), and the name of the new, sorted file to be created. The name you specify for the new file must follow the rules for all *dBase III* filenames.

Using the example list of names and addresses in Figure 7-1, you can create a new file sorted in ascending alphabetical order (*A–Z*) of last name with the following commands:

USE PEOPLE
SORT ON LAST /A TO PEOPLE2

This tells *dBase* to sort the file according to the contents of the field LAST, to arrange the records in ascending order (specified by /A) and to produce a new file called PEOPLE2. Since LAST is a character field, *dBase* sorts the file in ascending alphabetical order based on the data in that field. This process produces a new file but does not have any effect on the original; the records there remain intact.

To view the records in this new file and see the effect of the SORT command, enter

USE PEOPLE2
LIST

Note that there are now two files, PEOPLE and PEOPLE2, containing exactly the same records, but they are not in the same order. Notice that record numbers in this new file are now associated with different records. For example, the name which was record 8 in the original file PEOPLE now appears as record 7 in the sorted file PEOPLE2. This illustrates an important point about all data-management programs: It is not wise to identify records by their record number alone in order to locate them within a file. Many commands (such as SORT, PACK, and INSERT) can change record numbers, making it difficult to locate the record you need.

The SORT command can also order the records according to the contents of numeric or date fields, but not according to logical or memo fields. Note that if you do not specify what order the files are to be sorted into, *dBase III Plus* will sort files in ascending order. To arrange a file in descending order, follow the field name with /D:

SORT ON LAST /D TO PEOPLE3

An alternative using /A or /D is to include the words ASCENDING or DESCENDING after the field name. Keep in mind that *dBase III Plus* sorts character data by the ASCII value of the character codes, which places uppercase (capital) letters before lowercase. In other words, *dBase* would consider the following list properly sorted, since the words which begin with uppercase letters are placed before those beginning with lowercase:

Allan
George
Raymond
bob
steve
william

In most cases, you'll want a file arranged in a standard *A*-to-*Z* order, regardless of the case of the letters. By following the field name in a SORT command with /C, you instruct *dBase* to ignore differences in case. The /C is combined with /A or /D by using a single slash, as in /DC.

SORT ON LAST /DC TO PEOPLE3

will ignore case differences and alphabetize the current data file in Z-to-*A* order.

Sorting on Multiple Fields

In some situations, multiple levels of sorting are required. For example, you may need to sort a large name-and-address file by state and have all of the records within each state arranged alphabetically by last name. Combining field names in the SORT command accomplishes this.

SORT ON STATE/D,LAST/AC TO MAILFILE

This command creates a file called MAILFILE, arranged in descending alphabetical order by state. Those records which all belong to the same state are further alphabetized in ascending order by the last name, with any case differences ignored.

Limitations to Using SORT

Since the SORT command actually creates a new file, a certain amount of free disk space is required. If a file is sorted in its entirety, a file of equal size will be created. If disk space is at a premium, the SORT command may not be the best choice.

In addition, if records in a sorted file are edited, or if new records are added, the order is no longer assured. Another sort would be necessary to reorganize the file, to put new or changed records in their proper places.

Indexing

A more flexible technique for maintaining record order is the INDEX command. Indexing differs from sorting in two major ways. First, indexing does not physically alter the order of records in the data file. Instead, it creates a second file (an *index file*) which controls the order in which records in the main file appear. Secondly, indexing is dynamic, which means the data file will stay in the desired order even when new records are added or existing ones are changed.

To create an index which will arrange our PEOPLE file by last name, enter:

INDEX ON LAST TO NAMES

This creates an index file called NAMES.NDX which controls the order of the records in the data file PEOPLE. Since the LAST field was specified as the index *key,* information held in that field is used to establish record order.

Notice that the record numbers now seem to appear in random order, although they are still attached to the same records as they were before the index was built. In fact, the data file is unchanged; the index merely controls the order in which the records are displayed.

In this case, the top of the file is no longer record 1, nor is the bottom of the file record 11. To reach the first record in the file as established by the index, use the GO TOP command. Similarly, to reach the last record in the file, enter GO BOTTOM. When an index is active, the file appears in a logical order, as opposed to the physical order of the records themselves.

Likewise, the SKIP command behaves differently with an indexed file than it would with an unindexed file. Rather than moving the record pointer in record-number order, SKIP moves through the file in the order established by the index. In a further section, you'll see how this makes working with large files easier and more efficient.

Compound Indices

Index keys can also be comprised of multiple fields. For example:

INDEX ON STATE + CITY

arranges a file in an order established by the contents of the field STATE, and further organizes records within a given state in order by city.

You can create indices that will arrange a file in almost any imaginable order. Even though the INDEX command does not have the /D, /C, or /A options available with SORT, you can accomplish the same things without those options. For example, to arrange a file of inventory items in descending order in price (with the most expensive items first rather than last) you can create an index with the following command:

INDEX ON (PRICE * −1) TO HIGHCOST

Here, the index key is taken from the numeric value of the field PRICE multiplied by −1, which makes it into a negative number. The value stored in PRICE is unaffected, and the index is built on the result of the calculation PRICE * −1. The effect is the same as sorting in descending order.

To create an index which organizes a file by a character field, but one that does not distinguish between upper- and lowercase letters, use the UPPER( ) or LOWER( ) functions to convert the index key to all upper- or lowercase. This will have no effect on data in the file—no upper- or lowercase letters will actually be converted; it simply causes the index to behave as though all of the letters in the field were of the same case:

INDEX ON UPPER(LASTNAME) TO NAME

Once created, an index file automatically responds to changes in the data file which results from additions, deletions, and edits. The order established by the index file remains intact regardless of modifications to the data file itself. In order for an index file to maintain this order, however, it must be active whenever the data file is changed in any way. To open an index file when a data file is already active, enter:

SET INDEX TO indexname

An index file can also be specified when opening a file, as in:

USE PEOPLE INDEX NAMES

In order to USE or SET an index file, the index must have already been created with the INDEX command.

If a data file is opened and modified (edited, added to, packed, or deleted from) without having its associated index made active with SET or USE, the relationship between the index and data file will become *corrupted*, making the index unable to control the record order correctly. A corrupted index file can cause a wide variety of problems, many of which are far removed from improper record order. Records which you are certain are in the file may be inaccessible, or the file may appear scrambled and beyond salvaging.

Fortunately, the damage is usually less severe than it appears. Simply issuing the command REINDEX if the index is active may fix the problem, or you may have to recreate the index file by using the command INDEX ON *key* TO *indexfilename*. This will build a new index file from the ground up.

Tip: Whenever *dBase III Plus* behaves oddly, check for a corrupted index file first. Some of the symptoms of index corruption are so far removed from the underlying cause that you may never suspect index damage, although it is often at the root of many problems.

Multiple Indices

dBase III Plus allows you to create and maintain multiple indices on a single data file. This enables you to maintain a file in several different orders, and switch between them rapidly. *dBase III Plus* allows you to have up to seven active index files for a single active data file.

You may wish to maintain two indices on a customer file; one by the NAME field and another by the CUS_NUM (customer-number) field. The indices are created in the normal way and are made active together by entering

SET INDEX TO NAME, CUS_NUM

Since NAME was specified first, this index is established

as index 1, while CUS_NUM becomes index 2. Initially, index 1 controls the file order and thus the way it appears during an edit. (Both indices are updated with any changes made to the data file, provided they are both active.) To change the index priority so the file appears in order of customer number, enter

SET ORDER TO 2

To return to NAME order, enter

SET ORDER TO 1

If you use multiple indices with a data file, be certain that they are all active before making any changes to the file.

Locating Information in a Database File

A key feature of *dBase III Plus* is its ability to locate specific records within a file. Several methods for finding records are available, each with their own advantages and limitations.

The LOCATE Command

The simplest way of locating a record within a file is to use the LOCATE command. LOCATE works with every kind of field except memo fields, although its use differs slightly from one field type to another. LOCATE compares a value supplied by the user with the contents of a specified field within the data file. When a record which matches the supplied value is found, the user is notified. The basic syntax of the LOCATE command is:

LOCATE FOR <fieldname> = <value>

For example:

LOCATE FOR ID_NUMBER = 100

instructs *dBase III Plus* to search the numeric field ID_NUMBER in the active data file for a record which contains the number 100. *dBase III Plus* stops at the first record matching this condition and positions the record pointer at this record number. Thus, the matching record becomes the current record.

The value to which the field entry is being compared must be of the same type as the field itself (numeric, character, date, or logical). If the comparison data is different, a *Data type mismatch* error will occur.

If TALK is SET ON, *dBase III Plus* will respond to a successful LOCATE by displaying the record number onscreen, and will respond to an unsuccessful LOCATE with the message *End of Locate scope.* This means the end of the file was reached without finding a matching record. If TALK is set OFF, nothing is displayed. In this case, use the DISPLAY command or the FOUND( ) function to discover if a match was found. When using *dBase III Plus* interactively, it is usually better to leave TALK ON.

Unless told otherwise, LOCATE begins searching at the beginning of the active data file, and it will stop at the first record that matches the specified condition. Entering LOCATE a second time will start the process over and find the same record again. To find the second, third, or subsequent records that match the LOCATE condition, you would use the CONTINUE command. CONTINUE starts at the current position of the record pointer and stops at the next record that matches the LOCATE condition, or at the end of the file if no further matches are found. The following command sequence identifies all of the records in a file which have 100 as the contents of a field called ID_CODE:

```
LOCATE FOR ID_CODE = 100
 RECORD = 7
CONTINUE
 RECORD = 16
CONTINUE
 RECORD = 27
CONTINUE
 End of LOCATE scope
```

The responses show that record numbers 7, 16, and 27 contain 100 in the ID_CODE field.

The previous examples show how LOCATE can be used to find records by searching for an exact match. *dBase III Plus* also allows you to find records which are greater than or less than an exact match. For example, you can instruct *dBase III Plus* to find the first record in which the field PRICE contains a value greater than 75:

LOCATE FOR PRICE >75

With numeric fields, many types of comparisons are possible. For example,

LOCATE FOR PRICE <= 30

looks for a record in which the value in the PRICE field is less than or equal to 30.

LOCATE FOR PRICE <> 50

or

LOCATE FOR PRICE # 50

finds the first record in which the value in the PRICE field is *not* equal to 50.

It is also possible to compare the contents of one field to the contents of another with the LOCATE command:

LOCATE FOR ON_HAND <= MINIMUM

locates the first record in which the value in the ON_HAND field is less than or equal to the value in the MINIMUM field.

Locating with Character Fields

LOCATE is used most often with character fields. Character data being compared to the contents of a character field must be enclosed in quotes. This informs *dBase III Plus* that the value you are searching for is a string of characters and not the name of a field or memory variable.

LOCATE FOR LASTNAME = "SMITH"

searches the file for the first record in which the LASTNAME field contains SMITH. If the quotation marks were omitted, *dBase* would have assumed that SMITH is the name of a memory variable or of another field in the file.

dBase III Plus is *case-sensitive,* which means that it will accept a record as a match only if the characters are in the same case (upper- or lowercase) as the value to which they are being compared. In the above example, a record containing *SMITH* in the LASTNAME field would be found, but one containing *Smith* would not. To get around this limitation, use the UPPER( ) or LOWER( ) functions to convert the contents of the field to a uniform case. These functions do not actually change the field contents; they merely make the field appear in the specified format during the comparison.

LOCATE FOR UPPER(LASTNAME) = "SMITH"

or

LOCATE FOR LOWER(LASTNAME) = "smith"

will both find *Smith, SMITH, smith,* or even *SmItH.*

If you need to locate a record but do not know the exact contents or spelling of what you are looking for, use the SET EXACT OFF command. For example, suppose you need to locate a person's name-and-address record, but you are unsure of the spelling of the name. The SET EXACT OFF command allows you to search for records by using only the first part of a character field. With SET EXACT OFF, the following command:

LOCATE FOR LASTNAME = "SMI"

will find SMITH, SMITHERS, or SMILEY.

Notice that an EXACT OFF search will find only matches of characters starting on the left side of the field. The SMI in DISMISS would pass unnoticed by *dBase*. With SET EXACT ON, only an exact match (a record containing SMI alone in the LASTNAME field) would be found.

dBase III Plus also provides a means of finding records in which a character field contains information in an unknown position. For example, a 50-character-wide description field for an inventory item might contain the following entry:

PLIERS, NEEDLENOSE—6" LENGTH

Trying to find this record would present a problem if you were searching for needlenose pliers. One approach is to use the $ operator, which means *is contained within*. For example:

LOCATE FOR "NEEDLENOSE" $ UPPER(DESCRIP)

says: Locate a record in which the character sequence NEEDLENOSE is contained within an uppercase view of a field named DESCRIP.

The $ operator can also be used in reverse; it will determine whether the contents of a field are contained within a sequence of characters. If a file had a one-character-wide field called DEPARTMENT, you could locate a record in which that field contained either *B, D,* or *N* with the following command:

LOCATE FOR DEPARTMENT $ "BDN"

Date Comparisons

When using LOCATE with date fields, you can't enter a date directly from the keyboard. Information from the keyboard must be character data (enclosed in quotation marks), field names, memory variables, or numeric data. To enter a date, you must enter it as a string of characters and process it with the CTOD( ) (character-to-date conversion) function:

LOCATE FOR BIRTHDAY = CTOD("09/06/85")

Like numeric comparisons, date comparisons can include greater-than and less-than operators (in any combination) to test for dates before or after a specific date:

LOCATE FOR EXP_DATE <= DATE( )

locates the first record whose EXP_DATE field contains a date before or the same as today's date, which is returned by the DATE( ) function.

For the DATE( ) function to return a proper value for today's date, the date in the computer's operating system must be accurate. Today's date is set at boot-up, or set by automatic-clock hardware built into the computer. Consult your DOS manual for more information on using and setting the system date.

Logical Fields

Since logical fields can contain only one of two possible entries (true or false), they are less common in LOCATE operations. Nevertheless, logical fields can be used as part of a LOCATE condition and tested much like any other field.

The syntax for comparisons with logical fields is somewhat different from that used with numeric, character, or date fields.

To locate a record in which the contents of the field IS_MEMBER is true, you merely enter

LOCATE FOR IS_MEMBER

It is important to know that *dBase* stops reading a command after it has read a logical field name. Entering LOCATE FOR IS_MEMBER = .T. would have the same effect as the command above only because *dBase III Plus* ignores everything after the field name IS_MEMBER. Using the command in this way is a common trap that causes unwanted results:

LOCATE FOR IS_MEMBER = .F. (incorrect)

Although this command seems correct, it actually has just the opposite effect of what is intended. It will report .T. values for the field, not .F. values. Since *dBase* knows that IS_MEMBER is logical, it ignores everything after the field name and simply locates a record in which IS_MEMBER is true.

To properly locate a record in which IS_MEMBER has a false value in it, enter:

LOCATE FOR .NOT. IS_MEMBER

The next section will cover the use of logical operators like .NOT.

Logical Operators

Many *dBase III Plus* commands, including LOCATE, allow logical operators to be used in order to expand their capabilities. The three basic logical operators—.AND., .OR., and .NOT.—can combine several comparisons into a single command. For example, to locate a record in which the contents of the PRICE field is greater than 50 but less than 100, use

LOCATE FOR PRICE > 50 .AND. PRICE < 100

PRICE is specified twice, since the command actually consists of two separate comparisons joined by .AND. Both comparisons must be true for a find to be reported. Note the periods surrounding the word AND; these are necessary to identify the word as a logical operator.

The .OR. operator allows you to identify records which meet at least one of several conditions. To find a record in which the STATE field is either RI or CT, you would enter:

LOCATE FOR STATE = "RI" .OR. STATE = "CT"

Similarly, the .NOT. operator identifies records in which a specific condition is not true. The .NOT. operator is usually used to locate or display records according to the contents of a logical field, but it will work with other field types as well.

LOCATE FOR .NOT. (STATE="RI" .OR. STATE="CT")

will locate records in which the STATE field is *neither* RI nor CT. Notice the use of the parentheses to group logical operators together. If there were no parentheses in the above example, *dBase* would locate records in which STATE either *is not* RI or STATE *is* CT.

Limiting the Scope of LOCATE

You can limit the action of the LOCATE command. You may limit the action of the command to a certain range of records, or start the command at the current record-pointer position rather than at the beginning of the file. The commands which affect LOCATE scope are NEXT <n>, REST, and WHILE.

NEXT <n> begins LOCATE at the current record and searches only the specified number of following records:

LOCATE FOR ID_CODE = 123 NEXT 25

Only the current record and the 24 records following it will be searched by this LOCATE command.

REST is similar, informing LOCATE to begin searching at the current position of the record pointer, but to search records to the end of the file.

WHILE is a powerful *dBase III Plus* scope command that is covered in detail in the section devoted to dealing with large files. WHILE causes a command (in this case LOCATE) to perform its operation if a certain condition holds true for a record. If the condition specified by the WHILE clause is not true, the command skips the record.

LOCATE FOR NAME = "SMITH" WHILE STATE = "RI"

limits the LOCATE scope to records which have RI in the STATE field. If the record does not have RI in the STATE field, LOCATE will not report a find.

FIND and SEEK

Since LOCATE examines every record from the start of a data file until it finds a match, it can be very time consuming if large data files are involved. By creating an index on a key field, you are able to use the FIND and SEEK commands to locate records in a fraction of the time required for the LOCATE command. FIND and SEEK do not become slower as the file size grows; they are able to find records as quickly in a very large file as they are in a small one. Both commands require an active index in order to work; issuing either command without an active index returns an error message.

A typical use of the FIND command is

```
USE PEOPLE INDEX LASTNAME
FIND SMITH
  Record = 45
```

Notice that the FIND command does not require that character strings be enclosed in quotation marks, as do the LOCATE or SEEK commands. In addition, notice that the field LASTNAME which may hold the character string SMITH did not have to be specified. When an index is established, it is established on a key field. It is on this key field that the search is conducted.

The FIND command can be used to rapidly position the record pointer at a particular section of the data file. For example, to position the record pointer on the first record with a LASTNAME beginning with *H*, enter:

FIND H

This technique allows you to quickly find the records in the file beginning with *H*. This command will work only with EXACT set to OFF; setting EXACT ON requires you to enter an exact match.

As with the LOCATE command, the SET TALK [ON/OFF] command turns on and off messages to the screen about the success of a search. With TALK ON, an unsuccessful FIND results in the message *No find.*

SEEK is similar to FIND, but allows searching for data using *dBase* functions rather than literal comparisons. To use SEEK to find the first record in which the date field BIRTHDAY is January 12, 1959, enter

SEEK CTOD("01/12/59")

Limitations to FIND and SEEK

Both FIND and SEEK rely on index files to locate records, so it is essential that the active index be intact; a corrupted index may result in a record not being found even though it actually is in the data file.

Since both the FIND and SEEK commands use indices, any search must then use two files—the index and the file which is indexed—to find data. Since it takes as much time to look through the index to a small file as it does to look through the index of a large file, search time will be no longer for a long file than for a short one. As a result, SEEK and FIND will be faster than LOCATE with a search through a long file, but slower than LOCATE in searching a short file. With larger files, the time required to look into the index and then position the record pointer in the data file is far shorter than the time that would be required to find a record with the LOCATE command. With small files the LOCATE command can actually be faster since it reads from only one file, the data file itself.

Several of the options available with the LOCATE command are not supported by FIND and SEEK. One such option is the $ operator, which finds one string of characters inside another. Only fields which exactly match a sought-for string or fields which match a sought-for string starting at the leftmost character of the field can be found with the FIND or SEEK command. Searches which need to find a match in the middle of a field cannot be carried out. The NEXT and REST options are also unavailable with FIND and SEEK, but they are not needed in most cases. Since the file must be indexed, all of the records which match the search criteria specified in the FIND or SEEK command will be organized together, making the CONTINUE command unnecessary as well. For more information, see the section of this book devoted to handling large data files.

Using a *Filter* gives you an alternative to LOCATE, FIND, or SEEK. When a filter is defined and activated, the data file appears to contain only the records you are interested in, although the file itself remains physically unchanged.

For example, you may wish to list, edit, or just browse through only those records in your mailing list file in which the STATE field contains NY. The command

SET FILTER TO STATE = "NY"

makes the file seem as though only those records are present.

Commands such as LIST, EDIT, or COUNT will reveal only those records which match the filter template, and reports or mailing labels will also include only those records.

If a filter is active, its definition will appear when you issue the DISPLAY STATUS command.

All of the processes that go on behind the scenes and the execution times for commands (such as searching through the data file with LOCATE or DISPLAYing only certain records) remain unchanged when a filter is active. For this reason, some operations may seem slow; the apparent sluggishness comes from the false impression that the data file contains only records matching the filter. In fact, the entire file is still involved in all operations, and any commands which were slow with no filter active will be just as slow with a filter in place.

Using Views

Active data files, their associated indices, a filter condition, a field list, and relations between files (discussed in detail in another section) can all be thought of as one related group. *dBase III Plus* allows you to refer to a complete set of operating conditions as a *view.* For example, you may open a file of names and addresses, establish an index by last name and another by zip code, open a format file, and establish a filter showing only records for one state. To recreate this environment each time you enter the system would require many steps. The VIEW command allows you to save the operating environment and establish it as needed later on.

To use the VIEW command, enter

CREATE VIEW <filename>

dBase III Plus will then place you into a full-screen, menu-driven environment where you can select the data file or files you wish included in this view, along with associated indices, fields, and file relations. Selecting SAVE from the EXIT option on the menu creates a view file with the name <filename>.VUE which contains the information needed to recreate this particular set of operating conditions later on. The name you select for the view file must follow the same file-naming conventions used for data, index, or format files; no more than eight characters in length, no special characters, and so on.

To activate a view after it has been created, enter

SET VIEW TO <filename>

dBase III Plus will establish all of the conditions which were present when the view was created or last modified.

An alternate method for creating a view is first to set the operating environment as you wish it to be directly from the dot prompt. Next, save this view to a view file (with the extension .VUE) with the following command:

CREATE VIEW <filename> FROM ENVIRONMENT

This creates the view file directly from the conditions in place, and insures you that the exact conditions you want saved are included in the view.

Working with Large Files

All *dBase III Plus* commands work with both large and small files, but certain techniques are much more efficient when the file size grows beyond a few hundred records.

The Importance of Indexing

With larger files, indexing becomes much more important. Performing a SORT on a large file is both slow and wasteful of disk space, since a SORT produces a new data file that is as large as the original. Indexing requires far less storage space, is much faster, and maintains file order even if changes are made to the file.

An even more important aspect of indexing is the ability to use the FIND and SEEK commands to find specific records. Both FIND and SEEK must be used with an indexed file. The time required to FIND or SEEK a record remains constant as file size grows; the average time required to LOCATE a record grows proportionately with the file size. The difference is more acute if the record you are looking for is positioned near the end of the file. Both FIND and SEEK will jump to the record immediately, while LOCATE will view every record in the file starting with the first, until it reaches the one you are looking for.

WHILE and FOR

Generally, FOR is used with a command which performs a repeated task, such as searching a field for a specific value; WHILE performs a task only if a certain condition holds true. Proper use of the WHILE clause becomes far more important in large files than it does with smaller ones. Combined with properly designed index files, WHILE can make a large file respond to almost every command quickly. Consider a large file of inventory information. To get a count of the number of records in the file which have *HAMMER* in the DESCRIPTION field, you could enter

COUNT FOR DESCRIPTION = "HAMMER"

dBase III Plus would then scan the data file from beginning to end and count the number of records which match the comparison—a potentially slow process. A much more efficient method is to first organize the file by description with an index:

INDEX ON DESCRIPTION TO DESCRIP

This index serves two purposes. First, it keeps together all records which have the same contents in a given field, so that they can be processed as a group. Secondly, it permits use of the FIND or SEEK commands to reach the desired section of the file quickly:

FIND HAMMER

If the file contains a record in which the field DESCRIPTION contains *HAMMER*, this will place the record pointer on the first record which matches. Since the condition DESCRIPTION = "HAMMER" is now true, use the WHILE clause:

COUNT WHILE DESCRIPTION = "HAMMER"

WHILE begins at the current position of the record pointer, and stops as soon as the condition is no longer true; in this case it stops when it encounters the first record in which DESCRIPTION does not contain *HAMMER*. The COUNT process does not continue the time-consuming process of searching to the end of the file, as it would with a FOR command. Note that it was necessary to position the record pointer to a matching record *first*, or the WHILE clause would prevent the COUNT command from executing at all.

When a WHILE condition is true, you can still test for other conditions with the FOR clause.

COUNT WHILE DESCRIPTION = "HAMMER" FOR VENDOR = "ACME"

will read the same limited number of records, but it will count only those which have *ACME* in the VENDOR field. The alternative command, COUNT FOR DESCRIPTION = "HAMMER" .AND. VENDOR = "ACME", would be much, much slower.

To summarize the basic steps in processing part of a large file:

1. Organize the file with an appropriate index.
2. Use FIND and SEEK to place the record pointer on a desired record.
3. Use WHILE to restrict command execution to the desired range.

These same techniques apply to almost every command,

and especially to those which produce output from the file, such as the REPORT and LABEL commands. You can use this technique to print mailing labels for only the state of New York from a large mailing list. This list has an index file STATE which is built on a field which has state names as contents:

USE MAILLIST INDEX STATE
FIND NY
LABEL FORM MAILING TO PRINT WHILE STATE = "NY"

Adding and Deleting Records

When deleting a record from a file, the record does not actually disappear; it is only marked for deletion. The actual deletion occurs when a PACK command is executed. When files are large and there will be a number of additions and deletions, it is not efficient to delete records, pack the file, and then append new records. A more logical approach is to mark unwanted records for deletion and then reclaim the space for new records.

For example, suppose record 1085 is unneeded, while another new record needs to be appended to the file. The most efficient use of space and time is to place the record pointer on record 1085, enter the EDIT mode, and replace the contents with the new record. If you need to remove the old record but do not yet have another record to take its place, simply delete the record (which only marks the record for deletion), SET DELETED ON, and consider it out of the way. Then, when a new record is ready to be added to the file, enter SET DELETED OFF (which makes deleted records visible), and locate the first deleted record with

LOCATE FOR DELETED( )

Next, reclaim the deleted record with RECALL, enter the EDIT mode, and replace the contents with new data. Of course, be certain that all related index files are active when performing any of these commands, or the index will be corrupted.

Backing Up Your Data

A data file represents a big investment of time and work. You should take care to protect all of your valuable data, no matter how large or small the file. With a large file, however, the potential for loss is greater, and more attention should be given to making backups of the data file. Operating a database system without making proper backups is like driving a car without a spare tire.

If you are using *dBase III Plus* on a system with a hard disk, you should make regular backups of your data files onto floppy disks. The disks should be stored in a safe place (away from the computer) and protected against physical damage. Floppy-disk users can make copies of their data files with the DISKCOPY command from DOS. Be sure that you use this command carefully and copy data from your data disks onto the backups, and not the other way around.

If you find the backup procedure to be too time consuming, consider investing in a high-speed tape backup unit. These are available from a number of different manufacturers, and many of these units can back up an entire 20-megabyte hard disk (data as well as program files) in less than five minutes. What's more, the price of these machines has dropped significantly in the past few years, making them less of a luxury and more like standard equipment.

Relational Functions

The ability to relate separate files elevates *dBase III Plus* above most other data-management programs. A relational database can handle data much more efficiently than a nonrelational (or *flat file)* program.

To understand relational operations, consider a file used to record sales. Each record in the file contains fields for the following data:

CUSTOMER NUMBER
CUSTOMER NAME
CUSTOMER ADDRESS
CUSTOMER CITY
CUSTOMER STATE
CUSTOMER ZIP
CUSTOMER PHONE
INVOICE DATE
INVOICE NUMBER
ITEM NUMBER
ITEM DESCRIPTION
QUANTITY
PRICE EACH
TAX
INVOICE TOTAL

Each time a sale is made, all of this information is recorded and put into the file. Although everything seems to be covered fairly well, this file design has a number of limitations.

First, the file does not make provision for more than one item per record. If a customer purchases several different items, a new record would be required for each. You could redesign the file and add more fields to accomodate several items per record. But if you do this, record space would be wasted when invoices have only one item, and there would not be enough space for invoices containing many items. In addition, such an arrangement makes it difficult to search the file for a particular item, since you can't be sure which field it might be in.

Fortunately, *dBase III Plus* allows you to connect—or *relate*—data files, providing a very elegent way around this dilemma. Start by rethinking your approach to the design of the file: An invoice will be more than a simple record; for a single invoice there will be one or more individual items involved. Therefore, this information can be stored in two separate files, one containing invoice information and the other holding information on the items sold. Our new approach to the storage task looks like this:

Invoice File	**Item File**
CUSTOMER NUMBER	INVOICE NUMBER
CUSTOMER NAME	ITEM NUMBER
CUSTOMER ADDRESS	ITEM DESCRIPTION
CUSTOMER CITY	QUANTITY
CUSTOMER STATE	PRICE EACH
CUSTOMER ZIP	
CUSTOMER PHONE	
INVOICE DATE	
INVOICE NUMBER	
TAX	
INVOICE TOTAL	

Now, each invoice record can have as many records as necessary in the item file. Notice that one field, INVOICE NUMBER (INV_NO) is the same in both files; this is necessary to link the files together. *There must be a common field,* or else there would be no way to identify which items belong to which invoice.

With this arrangement, the number of items is not limited to the number of fields on a single invoice record. Invoices with many items simply have more related records in the item file; those with few items do not waste storage space.

This file structure is often called a *one-to-many relation,* since there are many item records for one invoice record. Another term often used is *parent-to-child,* with the invoice file viewed as the parent, and the item file viewed as the child.

Using Multiple Files

Until now, we have dealt with only one data file at a time. With related files, it becomes necessary to have two or more files open at the same time. *dBase III Plus* allows up to ten files to be open at once, although it is very unlikely that you would ever need this many.

Working with multiple files is accomplished by choosing alternate work areas with the SELECT command. When *dBase III Plus* is first started, work area 1 is used by default. Every time you open (or USE) a file, any other file that was open in the same work area is automatically closed. There can be only one file open in any one area at the same time. However, you can open a second file in another area while a file remains open in the first area. Using the example of an invoice file and an item file, open both files in this way:

SELECT 1	(Choose work area 1)
USE INVOICE	(Open the first file)
SELECT 2	(Switch to another work area)
USE ITEMS	(Open the second file)

Now you can use both files independently, since each is in its own separate working environment. To process the file in work area 1, enter any of the following:

SELECT 1

or

SELECT A

or

SELECT INVOICE

Notice that a work area can be referred to in many ways: by the name of the file which is currently open in that area, by the numbers 1–10, or by the letters *A–J*. This is the reason *dBase III Plus* does not allow data files to have names which are only one character in length; it would cause confusion when using multiple work areas.

When working within a given work area, the USE command affects only that work area. For example, typing USE alone while in work area 1 will close the invoice file but leave the item file active in work area 2.

Each work area has its own record pointer which can be moved independently of the record pointer in other areas. Moving the record pointer to a given record in one work area does not affect the position of the pointer in another area.

Establishing Relationships Between Files

Although the work areas can be used independently, it is more useful if they are linked—or *related*—in some way. In the case of our invoice- and item-file example, you want to have access to records in the item file while using the invoice file. This way, you can see which items are included in a given invoice.

The SET RELATION command allows files in separate work areas to be linked together. For this command to work, the file which is being *related into* must be indexed by the common field, in this case INV_NO. The index allows *dBase* to position the record pointer in the item file automatically whenever the record pointer in the invoice file is moved. The steps for establishing this relation are

```
SELECT 1                              (Choose first work area)
USE INVOICE INDEX INVOICE             (Open parent file and index)
SELECT 2                              (Choose alternate work area)
USE ITEMS INDEX INV_NO                (Open child file and index)
SELECT 1                              (Reselect work area 1)
SET RELATION TO INV_NO INTO ITEMS     (Establish relation)
```

At this point, the current file is in work area 1 (INVOICE), and a relationship exists which causes the record pointer in work area 2 to be repositioned automatically whenever the record pointer in work area 1 is moved.

Since SET RELATION TO INV_NO was specified, *dBase III Plus* uses the contents of the INV_NO field in work area 1 and, in effect, performs a SEEK on the file in work area 2. Moving the pointer in work area 1 in any way (GO, SKIP, LOCATE, and so on) also affects the pointer in area 2.

Because the item file is also indexed by Invoice Number, all of the records which correspond to a given invoice will be grouped together. When the record pointer is repositioned by the relation, it will always be positioned at the first record in the group of matching records in the related file. Observe the following illustration to see how this looks.

Figure 7-2. How Two Files are Related by Invoice Number

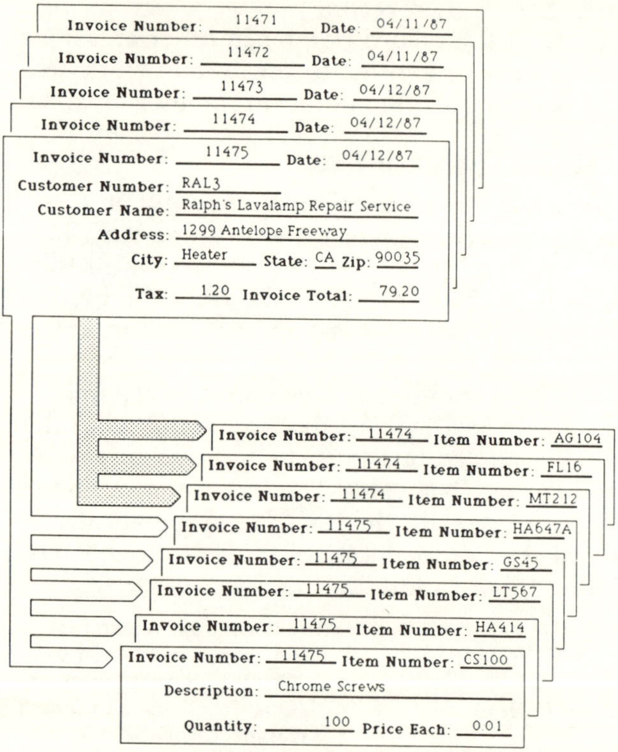

If for some reason the active record in work area 1 contains a value that does not correspond to a record in work area 2 (for example, if an invoice did not have any items on it), the record pointer in work area 2 is set to an end-of-file condition. Looking at work area 2 will reveal a blank record.

Viewing the Contents of Another Work Area

It would be possible, but very tedious, to switch back and forth between work areas each time you wish to view the current record. It is not necessary to do this because *dBase III Plus* provides a method of displaying data from a work area different from the one currently selected. By preceding a field name with either the filename, work-area number, or work-area letter and a dash followed by a greater-than symbol (together these make up a right arrow), you can specify which work area the data should be taken from. For example:

```
SELECT A
LOCATE FOR INV_NO = '10011'
DISPLAY B->ITEM_NO
```

In this case, the record pointer is positioned at the desired record in work area 1 (the Invoice file) with the LOCATE command. Assuming that the relationship between this file and the item file in work area 2 is properly established with a SET RELATION command, the record pointer in that file will be positioned accordingly. To see the first item number which was purchased on this invoice, you need to view the field ITEM_NO from the Items file in work area 2. This field can be referred to in three different ways:

```
B->ITEM_NO
2->ITEM_NO
ITEMS->ITEM_NO
```

Each of these identification codes (B, 2, or ITEMS) is known as an *alias* of the ITEMS file. If you wish, you can specify an alias that is different from the filename at the time you first open (or USE) the file. For example, if the following command is used to open the INVOICE file:

```
USE INVOICE INDEX INVOICE ALIAS SALES
```

you could then refer to the file as SALES rather than INVOICE.

Viewing Multiple Related Records

Once the record pointer in work area 2 is positioned properly, you want access to the entire group of records which belongs to the parent invoice record. This is necessary in order to list line items from the invoice or to total the prices of the individual items. One way to do this is to locate the proper record in work area 1 and then select work area 2 for displaying or totaling a group of records. The display command used in work area 2 would have to be limited in some way to include only those records which correspond to the parent record in work area 1:

```
SELECT INVOICE
LOCATE FOR INV_NO = '10011'
SELECT ITEMS
DISPLAY WHILE INV_NO = INVOICE->INV_NO
```

This command tells *dBase III Plus* to display records in the item file which have an invoice number matching the current record in the invoice file.

Turning the Relation Around

A file relation can be established in the other direction as well, linking records in the child file to those in the parent file. In this way, you can search through the item file for a particular record and still have access to data held in the appropriate record in the invoice file.

```
SELECT 1                                  (Choose first work area)
USE INVOICE INDEX INVOICE                 (Open parent file and index)
SELECT 2                                  (Choose alternate work area)
USE ITEMS INDEX INV_NO                    (Open child file and index)
SET RELATION TO INV_NO INTO INVOICE       (Establish relation into parent file)
```

Now, a command such as LOCATE FOR DESCRIP = "PLIERS" could be used to find the appropriate item record, and *dBase III Plus* will position the record pointer in work area 1 (Invoices) on the proper record automatically. If the LOCATE was successful, you can see who bought the pliers by entering

```
DISPLAY INVOICE->CUST_NAME
```

Relational Files in Reports

Information from a related file can be incorporated into a report or label as easily as it can be viewed onscreen. To design a report which pulls information from two separate files you must first open the files and establish the relations as shown above.

Once these are in place, you can use data from a related file in a report column or label simply by preceding the field name by the file alias and the arrow sign. A typical use for this would be to use the record in the parent file to group records in the child file. For example, printing a report of items, indexed by item number (ITEM_NO)—which is the field common to both files—recreates the original invoice format of a header and several line items.

Making One File from Two

Many relational operations can be performed with all of the data residing in separate files. At times, however, it is easier to join the contents of one file with that of another, making a new data file in the process.

The JOIN command produces a single database file from selected records and fields (except memo fields) of two other open files. To use JOIN, you must first open the two files that are to be joined:

```
SELECT 2
USE ITEMS
SELECT 1
USE INVOICE
JOIN WITH B TO ACTIVITY FOR INV_NO = B->INV_NO
```

Going Further

Now that you have an understanding of the basic principals involved in relational database theory, let's look again at our invoice file and see if it can be made still more efficient.

In most situations, one customer may make many purchases, just as one purchase may be comprised of many individual items. It is redundant to record the same customer's name, address, and so forth, each time he or she makes a purchase. It is much more efficient to record this information once, and access it as needed. Since each customer has a unique customer number (which is called CUST_NUM in our file), include this number with each invoice record and use this to link with a customer file:

Customer File	Invoice File	Item File
CUSTOMER NUMBER →	CUSTOMER NUMBER	INVOICE NUMBER
CUSTOMER NAME	INVOICE NUMBER ↗	ITEM NUMBER
CUSTOMER ADDRESS	INVOICE DATE	ITEM DESCRIPTION
CUSTOMER CITY	TAX	QUANTITY
CUSTOMER STATE	INVOICE TOTAL	PRICE EACH
CUSTOMER ZIP		
CUSTOMER PHONE		

Notice how a single record in the customer file can be linked to one or more records in the invoice file, each corresponding to a single sale. In turn, each record in the invoice file can have one or many corresponding records in the item file. The customer file and the invoice file are linked by the common field CUSTOMER NUMBER, and the invoice file and the item file are linked by the common field INVOICE NUMBER. This arrangement allows a great deal of flexibility, and increases the number of records that can be stored in the system by reducing wasted space.

A further step would be to create a separate inventory file to store the item number, description, and price for each item in stock. Then, the items file would only need to hold the item number, quantity, and invoice number; price and description would be taken from the inventory file.

Other Relational Applications

Some applications are clear candidates for multiple related files. For example, a professional time-and-billing system (as used by an attorney or consultant) would be comprised of separate files for Projects, Staff, and Time:

Projects		Time		Staff
PROJECT CODE	↘	DATE		EMPLOYEE CODE
PROJECT NAME		PROJECT CODE	↗	EMPLOYEE NAME
		EMPLOYEE CODE		BILLING RATE
		HOURS		

Each record in the Time file corresponds to a single transaction—a certain number of hours devoted to a particular project by one employee. In this way, any employee can work any amount of time on any project and the system will accommodate it. Reports can be produced to show activity by employee, by project, or for a given time period.

When are Relational Operations Needed?

Many, if not most, data-management tasks can be handled by a single data file. However, there are indications that show that a single file is not enough, and that a relational approach is needed. Any of the following is a red flag indicating that you should take a more careful look at the design of your data file:

- a large number of fields per record
- fields which are rarely, if ever, used
- records which don't seem to have enough fields
- several records in the same file containing the same basic information

- similar information stored in two or more fields of the same record
- not knowing exactly which field contains a given piece of information

Any of the above symptoms may have a cause other than poor file design, but encountering any of them should prompt you to look more closely at your approach.

Chapter 8

Creating Reports and Labels

Chapter 8

Creating Reports and Labels

A database program is only as good as the information it can provide. No matter how powerful a program may be in terms of adding, sorting, or locating records, it falls short of the mark if its ability to produce useful output is limited.

Making Reports from *dBase III Plus*

dBase III Plus has an extensive report generator that can produce any number of reports from the information in your data file. Once designed, a report is stored to disk as a report-format (.FRM) file so that it can be recalled and used at any time. The report design process is controlled by menus which allow complete control over the form, layout, and contents of each report.

In its simplest form, a report has columns of information, each corresponding to a field in the data file. At the top of each column is a user-specified heading to identify the column's contents.

Each record within the report appears as a separate row. The order of records within the report is determined by the order of records in the data file itself. Records will appear in record-number order unless an active index is controlling the record order in some other sequence.

Consider the following data file of inventory items:

#	ITEM_NO	TYPE	DESCRIP	COUNT	MIN	MAX	COST
1	H4201	HAMMER	BALLPEEN	24	21	63	3.79
2	H3410	HAMMER	CLAW	3	2	75	7.90
3	S1410	SCREW	¼″ #10	1200	200	2400	0.02
4	S1408	SCREW	¼″ #8	890	400	3000	0.02
5	S1406	SCREW	¼″ #6	425	250	900	0.01
6	N1410	NUT	¼″ #10	1000	500	2000	0.03
7	N1408	NUT	¼″ #8	560	750	4000	0.02
8	N1406	NUT	¼″ #6	400	100	500	0.02
9	W1801	WRENCH	⅛″ OPEN	7	3	9	3.23
10	W1402	WRENCH	¼″ OPEN	4	6	12	4.72

A report will give us the same information in a more pleasing and informative format. The *dBase* report generator can arrange the fields in any order, calculate the total of the values in numeric fields, group records together, and use descriptive headings. A heading such as Item Number or Product Description gives the user much more information than ITEM_NO or DESCRIP, which are only the field names of the entries in the columns.

It is important to grasp that the design of a report specifies how you want records displayed, but has nothing to do with selecting *which* records will be displayed, or in what *order* they will be displayed. Record selection and ordering must be handled before the report is produced; it is not part of the report design process.

Starting the Report Generator

The database (.DBF) file from which the report will be generated must first be opened with a USE command. You create report files with a command of the form

CREATE REPORT <filename>

If you wish to modify an existing report file rather than create a new file, use the command

MODIFY REPORT <filename>

For example, to create a new report file named STOCK, use the following command:

CREATE REPORT STOCK

This places you in the report-generator menu and allows the design of a report called STOCK.FRM.

Report Options

The first options menu in the report generator gives you control over such features as page length, margins, and spacing. The cursor up- and down-arrow keys move the highlighted bar to the various menu choices, and Enter selects the highlighted choice. With the menu bar on the Page Title menu item, press Enter. A window will appear with the cursor inside. The information you type in this window (from one to four lines) will appear at the top of the finished report and will be the report title.

For the example report, type

Acme Corporation
Inventory Status Report

Hardware Department

Remember to press Enter after each line. Press Enter alone to enter the blank third line. After pressing Enter on the last line, the window will close and you will return to the Options menu. If you want fewer than four lines in the heading, press Ctrl-End to return to the Options menu.

The information that you type in the Page Title window is automatically centered when the report is produced. An additional, one-line heading can appear at the very top of a report by specifying it at the time the report is produced.

The following menu options control report width, margins, and number of lines per page. The default values displayed are set for reports printed on standard, 8½ × 11–inch paper. If you were using a wide-carriage printer with 14-inch-wide paper, you would specify a page width of 130 characters. When page width is changed, the report heading will remain centered within the new margins. To change any of these values, simply highlight the appropriate menu choice, press Enter, type the new value, and press Enter once again.

Menu selections which have only *Yes* or *No* choices are changed from one to the other simply by pressing Enter. The *Page eject before printing* option allows you to choose whether the paper will advance to the top of the page before the first record is printed. The *Page eject after printing* option will eject a blank page after all printing is finished. If the *Plain page* option is set to *Yes,* the report heading is printed on the first page only, and the date and page number will be omitted altogether.

Report Groups

Next, move to the Groups menu with the cursor right-arrow key. In this menu you can select a particular field for grouping information together in the report. Whenever the value of the specified field changes, a blank line is printed and a new group is started. For the example report, we want to group the records in our inventory report according to the TYPE field. In this way, all of the kinds of hammers, kinds of screws, and other items will be printed together in their own group, with a blank line in between.

Select the *Group on expression* option with Enter and enter TYPE for the field name. On the next menu line, enter Item Type to serve as a group title. Note that this title, unlike the column heading, will be printed every time there is a change in the value of the TYPE field. A blank line will be printed before the line which shows the group title and group field name. See Figure 8-1 near the end of this chapter to see how this will look in a finished report.

It is important to realize that simply specifying here that a column will be grouped does not actually arrange the records together in a group. Grouping simply places blank lines between groups and allows an optional title or subtotal to be printed when the group expression changes. For this feature to work properly, the file must be arranged in the proper order to begin with, either by using the SORT or INDEX commands discussed in chapter 7. If records appear in the file in a random order, the group will change each time a different group expression is encountered, causing the report to appear jumbled and meaningless.

Other options in the Group menu allow you to specify a summary report, in which the individual records within a group are not displayed and only the number of records and any totals you specify are shown. Selecting *Page eject after group* causes the report to start a new page each time the group expression changes. This is more useful in large reports, and would be wasteful with a report in which all of the data could fit on a single page.

Within a group, you can break the report down further into subgroups. This is useful in situations where you have informatn such as inventory data grouped by type, and then further arranged by size or color within each type. Like the Group option, subgroups require the file to be arranged in the proper order prior to using the report form. See the section "Sorting on Multiple Fields" in chapter 7.

Column Definitions

With the next menu (Columns) you specify what data is to be printed, and where the data is to be printed in the report. A report can have any number of columns, each with its own heading and contents.

The first option within Columns is called Contents. This is where you specify what field will be printed in the column. In the example, use the field ITEM_NO for the contents of the first column. To do this, press Enter, type ITEM_NO, and press Enter again. Another option is to place the menu bar on Contents, press Enter, and then press F10. This brings up a list of fields in the data file, which can be useful if you have forgotten the exact title of a field name. Next, move the highlighted bar to the desired field and press Enter once more. This enters the field name into the Contents area, where you can accept it with another press of Enter.

Each column must contain either a field name from the data file, a derived value (such as the sum of one field added to another), or a constant. For example, you may wish to include a field in the stock report which shows the selling price of an item. This is calculated by multiplying the cost times 1½. To do this, simply create a column whose contents is COST * 1.5. The field COST itself does not have to be included anywhere in the report, but it must be a valid field in the database file. If the value you enter in the Contents section is invalid, *dBase III Plus* will display an error message and require you to reenter your selection.

The Heading menu option allows you to enter the text that you wish to appear above the column. Each heading can be from one to four rows in length, and may contain as much text as will fit in the column. Use Ctrl-End when you have entered what you want.

If the field expression is numeric, you can specify that column totals will be printed. A grand total will appear at the bottom of each totaled field in the report, and if grouping is specified, group subtotals will be printed for grouped numeric fields.

After entering the Contents expression, *dBase III Plus* automatically sets the field width to the length of the expression plus one character. If you enter a heading which is wider than the column width, the width is increased. If you need to make the column wider or narrower than the value shown, select Width from the Columns menu and then enter the desired value.

As you enter the field information, the report-format window at the bottom of the screen changes to show how the report will look when finished. The heading is shown in exactly the same format as it will appear in the final report, allowing you to edit it. Changes in column width are also shown, helping you choose the best settings. In this display, character fields are shown as a series of *X*'s, totaled numeric fields as #'s, and nontotaled numeric fields as 9s. Memo fields appear filled with *M*'s, date fields as *mm/dd/yy*, and Logical fields as *.L.*. At the far left of the report format, a series of greater-than signs (>) indicates the left margin setting. Increasing or decreasing the margin setting in the Options menu is reflected by a changing number of greater-than signs. Pressing PgDn moves you to the next column position in the report, and PgUp moves back to the previous field. As you move from field to field, the report-format section at the bottom of the screen shifts right and left so that you are always able to view the section of the report which holds the current field.

Locate, the next menu option, provides another means of moving from column to column within the report form. Selecting this option displays a list of column contents, with the leftmost columns at the top and those to the right, below. By highlighting any Contents selection and pressing Enter, the report generator will move to that field for editing. This is often faster than moving through the fields with PgUp and PgDn.

Adding and Deleting Report Fields

It is not uncommon to discover that a new report column is needed between two existing columns, or that a report column is not needed and must be deleted. Both situations are easily handled.

To insert a new report field between two existing columns, you may use the Locate option on the menu. Select the column that is to the right of where you want the new field to be inserted. Next, press Ctrl-N and a new column will be inserted into the report form. Until the contents or width of this column are specified, it will appear in the report-format section at the bottom of the screen as *?* .

To remove unwanted columns, select the field you wish to eliminate and press Ctrl-U—the same command used to delete records in full-screen operations.

Exit

When the report is finished, the Exit menu option allows you to leave the report generator and save your work. The Exit option also allows you to abandon operation and cancel the

Figure 8-1. A Finished Report

Page No. 1
05/05/87

Acme Corporation
Inventory Status Report
Hardware Department

Item Number	Product Description	Quantity In Stock	Cost Each	Selling Price
** Item type -> HAMMER				
H4201	BALLPEEN	24	3.79	5.69
H3410	CLAW	3	7.90	11.85
** Subtotal **				
		27		
** Item type -> SCREW				
S1410	¼″ #10	1200	0.02	0.03
S1408	¼″ #8	890	0.02	0.03
S1406	¼″ #6	425	0.01	0.02
** Subtotal **				
		2515		
** Item type -> NUT				
N1410	¼″ #10	1000	0.03	0.04
N1408	¼″ #8	560	0.02	0.03
N1406	¼″ #6	400	0.02	0.03
** Subtotal **				
		1960		
** Item type -> WRENCH				
W1801	⅛″ OPEN	7	3.23	4.84
W1402	¼″ OPEN	4	4.72	7.08
** Subtotal **				
		11		
*** Total ***				
		4513		

report design and modification process. The finished report will be saved in a file named *reportname*.FRM, where *reportname* is the name you specified in the CREATE/MODIFY REPORT command.

Using the Report

The command for activating a report is

REPORT FORM <reportname> [WHILE <CONDITION>] [FOR <CONDITION>] [TO PRINT/TO FILE <filename>] [PLAIN] [HEADING <heading>] [NOEJECT] [SUMMARY]

In the case of our example report, STOCK, the command to send this report to the printer would be

REPORT FORM STOCK TO PRINT

Using some of the examples given above, our report would look like Figure 8-1 on the previous page.

Selecting Records for the Report

Reports will include all records in the data file, beginning at the top of the file, unless a FOR and/or WHILE condition is specified. This is the way in which records are chosen for the report. To select for inclusion only those records which cost over $100, you could specify:

REPORT FORM STOCK TO PRINT FOR COST >100

In general, selecting records for a report follows the same rules as selecting records with any other command such as LIST or DISPLAY.

Command Options

PLAIN. The PLAIN option suppresses the report title, page number, and date from the top of a report. This allows a few more lines to fit on a single printed page.

NOEJECT. Normally, *dBase III Plus* ejects a sheet of paper before beginning a printed report. To suppress this waste of paper, specify NOEJECT in the report command. After the report has finished printing, issue the EJECT command to eject the finished product from the printer.

TO PRINT. Sends the report to the printer as well as to the screen. To suppress the screen display during printing, use the SET CONSOLE OFF command. Be certain to issue the command SET CONSOLE ON after the report is finished or no screen display will be visible. (The screen will not display this command while it is being entered.)

TO FILE <filename>. Sends the report to a disk file named <filename>, as well as to the screen. To suppress the screen display during file output, use the SET CONSOLE OFF command. Be certain to issue the command SET CONSOLE ON after the report is finished or no screen display will be visible. (The screen will not display this command while it is being entered.)

HEADING <text>. Specify a one-line string of text, <text>, to appear at the top of the report. If the text is typed directly from the dot prompt, it must be enclosed in quotes. The heading is suppressed if PLAIN is specified.

SUMMARY. Supresses individual line items from the report, and shows only subtotals and totals for specified groups.

Creating Additional Reports

Any number of report-format files can be created for a single data file. Each report resides on disk and occupies a relatively small amount of storage space.

You may wish to create a report that is very similar to another. For example, you may want one report called STOCK which shows product descriptions along with inventory levels and cost, and another report called PRODUCT which is essentially the same except that it suppresses inventory and cost data. Rather than design the second report from scratch, it is easier to create one report as you have done in this chapter, copy the design to a new report file, and modify the new report as necessary. For example:

COPY FILE STOCK.FRM TO PRODUCT.FRM
MODIFY REPORT PRODUCT

Making Mailing Labels

The *dBase III Plus* LABEL command makes it easy to create mailing labels from data in a file. The full-screen label design mode gives you control over the contents and format of almost any size mailing label.

To use the LABEL command, you must first open a data file with the USE command. If you issue the CREATE LABEL command without an open file, *dBase* will prompt you for the name of a data file. The syntax of the command is

CREATE LABEL <filename>

dBase will store the label definition in a file called <filename>.LBL, using the name you specify.

There are two parts to making labels: specifying the size of the label and specifying the contents.

You can choose the size of the label from several predefined formats, such as 3-1/2 × 15/16 (a standard mailing label), 4 × 1-7/16, and 3-2/10 × 11/12 (Cheshire). If you are using a nonstandard label, you can define your own combination of height, width, and number of labels across a page.

You must specify the fields you wish included in the finished label. Each line in the label is shown, and you can move up and down with the cursor keys to the desired position. A simple label definition to produce mailing labels from a mailing-list file looks like this:

1 FIRSTNAME,LASTNAME
2 ADDRESS
3 CITY,STATE,ZIP

dBase does not include the commas in the finished label; this simply tells the program to place the contents of the specified fields next to each other.

Any valid *dBase* function can be included in a label definition. This allows you to dress up the final product in a number of ways. For example, to print city, state, and zip code in a more traditional form—*city*(comma) *state zip*—enter line 3 of the label definition in this way:

3 TRIM(CITY)+", "+STATE,ZIP

Trailing spaces are removed from the CITY field with the TRIM( ) function, and a comma and a space are added, followed by the state and zip code. Text such as seasonal greetings or messages can be included in the label definition by enclosing it in quotes:

1 FIRSTNAME,LASTNAME
2 ADDRESS
3 CITY,STATE,ZIP
4 CHR(255)
5 "Season's Greetings"

Normally, *dBase* does not leave blank lines on a label. If the line is left blank, the items from below are moved up one row. However, there are times when you want a blank line on the label. A simple trick which will do this is shown above.

Putting an unprintable character such as CHR(255) on a line causes *dBase III Plus* to think the line is occupied, even though nothing will actually appear when it is printed.

To produce labels, enter:

LABEL FORM <.lbl filename> [<scope>] [WHILE <condition>] [FOR <condition>] [TO PRINT] [SAMPLE]

If TO PRINT is included, the labels will be sent to the printer as well as to the screen.

The SAMPLE option produces a label made up of asterisks (*) to aid in printer alignment prior to printing the actual data. If the asterisks do not fit within the label, adjust the form in your printer and respond with *Y* when asked *"Do you want more samples?* When the label aligns properly, answer the prompt with *N* and label printing will begin. Pressing the Esc key will interrupt the printing and return you to the dot prompt.

If you need to begin the label-printing process at a particular record, or need to resume printing after stopping, position the record pointer on the record you wish to begin with and use REST (or NEXT <n>) at the *scope* position in the LABEL FORM command shown above.

Beyond Labels

The *dBase III Plus* label feature can be used for more than just mailing labels. One use is making Rolodex-style cards for desktop phone directories, or printing membership cards on preprinted, continuous-form card stock. Experiment with different numbers for spacing and lines between labels and with different label heights until you get the information aligned properly.

Chapter 9

Using *dBase III Plus* with Other Software

Chapter 9

Using *dBase III Plus* with Other Software

As powerful and flexible as *dBase III Plus* may be, it cannot perform every task that personal computer users demand. A database program cannot be expected to do the work of word processors, spreadsheets, or graphics programs, each of which have their unique strengths. Still, there are times when the information-handling power of *dBase III Plus* needs to be combined with the special abilities of other programs. For example, you may wish to use a word processor to produce a form letter which includes the names and addresses found in a *dBase* mailing-list file. You may need to transfer files between *dBase* and *Lotus 1-2-3,* or you may need to bring information into *dBase III Plus* from another data-management program. To do this, you need a way of transferring information between *dBase III Plus* and other programs.

Transferring Data Between *dBase III Plus* and Other Programs

The problem with exchanging information with other programs lies in the fact that the other programs keep their information in files with different formats. *Lotus 1-2-3* spreadsheet files are not the same as *WordStar* document files, which are not the same as *dBase* database files. For this reason, information is usually passed to and from *dBase III Plus* and other programs by conversion to an intermediate format that can be read by both *dBase* and the other program. A number of data-interchange formats are in use, and *dBase III Plus* supports all of the most popular types.

Using Delimited ASCII Files

The most common data-transfer standard is the *ASCII delimited file.* In this format, information is stored character by character, with a delimiter (usually a comma) separating the fields. Quotes are placed around character data. Each record occupies a single line, with carriage-return and line-feed characters marking the end of each record.

A comma-delimited ASCII file containing names and addresses looks like this:

"Smith","Robert","127 Mill Road","Arlington","MA","02577"
"Hamilton","Beatrice"," ","North Bristol","CA","90455"

Note that there are commas between the fields, and that empty fields are included by the use of quotes with nothing in between. This is necessary to keep the fields in the proper order, so that information will not be placed in the wrong field. *dBase III Plus* allows you to create and read such files, making it possible to easily transfer between *dBase III Plus* and most other programs.

Sending Out Data

Consider a small file of company names and addresses which is to be used for mailings. The file structure is as follows:

Field	**Field Name**	**Type**	**Width**	**Dec**
1	COMPANY	Character	26	
2	ADDRESS	Character	23	
3	CITY	Character	15	
4	STATE	Character	2	
5	ZIP	Character	5	

Using the LIST command shows us the following records:

COMPANY	**ADDRESS**	**CITY**	**STATE**	**ZIP**
Greco Bros., Inc.	Greco Lane	Providence	RI	02909
Greenberg, B B Co.	333 West Street	Providence	RI	02904

To create a comma-delimited ASCII file from this information, use the COPY TO... command, which can generate several other file formats in addition to ordinary .DBF files. To create an ASCII delimited file which can be used by another program, use a command of the form

COPY TO <filename> DELIMITED

dBase III Plus will then produce a file called <filename>.TXT which contains the information in this format:

"Greco Bros., Inc.","Greco Lane","Providence","RI","02909"
"Greenberg, B B Co.","333 West Street","Providence","RI","02904"

This file can now be read directly by *WordStar* and many other popular programs, which can use this information to produce form letters and other personalized documents using the names and addresses in the *dBase* data file. Most word processing programs which support mail-merge functions make some provision for reading information from comma-delimited ASCII files. Like most *dBase III Plus* commands, the COPY TO command can limit the output to the ASCII file to only those records which meet set conditions. It can also send all fields in the record or just a few to the new ASCII file. This allows, for example, exporting only name-and-address information from a more detailed file. In addition, the COPY TO command allows you to specify the character you wish to use as a delimiter if the default comma and quotes aren't satisfactory. Examples of the available alternatives are as follows:

COPY TO <filename> DELIMITED WITH BLANK

creates an ASCII file with a single space separating the fields within each record.

COPY TO <filename> DELIMITED WITH / FIELDS NAME,ADDRESS,PHONE

creates an ASCII file with a slash (/) separating each field, and including information from the fields NAME, ADDRESS, and PHONE only.

Bringing Data into *dBase* Files

Reading information into *dBase III Plus* from an ASCII delimited file is just as easy, but requires some advance planning and proper design of the data file into which the information is to be stored.

Each field in the data file must be in the proper position, and must be large enough to contain the longest piece of information that will appear in that position. If the field is shorter than the entry that is brought into it, the excess characters will be lost.

If the file being loaded includes a field which is not needed in the *dBase III Plus* file, you must still designate a field in the *dBase* record to hold the incoming information, even if is only one character in length. After the information is loaded, the unwanted field can be removed from the data file using the MODIFY STRUCTURE command.

Once the new *dBase* data file is designed, or once an appropriate existing file is selected, you are ready to load the information. The command for bringing information into *dBase III Plus* from a comma-delimited ASCII file is

APPEND FROM <filename> DELIMITED

Records loaded in this way will be added to those already in the data file. If the delimiter is different from the default commas and quotes, it must be specified as DELIMITED WITH <delimiter>.

Both APPEND FROM and COPY TO support additional file formats. One example is the *SDF* (system data format) ASCII file. In this format, each field is of a definite specified length, and extra spaces are included to pad fields which contain data that is shorter than the field length. To create an SDF file from the above example, use the command

COPY TO <filename> TYPE SDF

which produces a file which looks like this:

```
Greco Bros., Inc.   Greco Lane         Providence RI02909
Greenberg, B B Co.  333 West Street    Providence RI02904
```

An SDF file can be read into *dBase III Plus* with the command

APPEND FROM <filename> TYPE SDF

in much the same way as a delimited file. Many mainframe and minicomputer systems transfer information in the SDF format. With the proper hardware connections and communications software, it is possible to share information between *dBase III Plus* and larger computer systems.

Using *dBase III Plus* with *Lotus 1-2-3*

In some cases, *dBase III Plus* makes provisions for reading and writing information in a format that is directly compatible with other programs. One example is *Lotus 1-2-3,* the very popular electronic spreadsheet program from Lotus Development Company. *dBase III Plus* allows you to directly read and write files compatible with Version 1A of *Lotus 1-2-3* (.WKS files).

Consider a worksheet with sales information for several different departments within a company:

	A	B	C	D
1	Monthly Sales Report			
2				
3	Department	Sales	Cost	Profit
4				
5	Commercial	2332.00	1492.48	839.52
6	Wholesale	6354.00	4066.56	2287.44
7	Retail	7645.00	4892.80	2752.20
8	International	3533.00	2261.12	1271.88

dBase III Plus can read this information into an existing data file. During the transfer process, each row in the spreadsheet is converted to a record within the data file, and each cell on a row is assigned to a field. Blank rows are eliminated, and *dBase III Plus* begins reading from the upper left corner of the worksheet, usually cell A1. By creating a data file with the following format:

Field	**Field Name**	**Type**	**Width**	**Dec**
1	DEPARTMENT	Character	15	
2	SALES	Numeric	7	2
3	COST	Numeric	7	2
4	PROFIT	Numeric	7	2

you can load the worksheet directly into the data file by typing

APPEND FROM <filename> TYPE WKS

Using the LIST command on the new data file shows the following:

Record#	DEPARTMENT	SALES	COST	PROFIT
1	Monthly Sales R			
2	Department	0	0	0
3	Commercial	2332.00	1492.48	
4	Wholesale	6354.00	4067.56	
5	Retail	7645.00	4893.80	
6	International	3533.00	2261.12	

Notice that no *dBase* records were created for rows 2 and 4 of the original *Lotus* spreadsheet because those rows were blank. Note also that only a portion of the worksheet caption, originally in cell A1, was captured in record 1 of the new data file. Only the characters that would fit in the first field were retained. The second record contain zeros in the numeric fields. This record was derived from row 3 of the original *Lotus* spreadsheet, which contained character-type information that could not be processed within a *dBase* numeric field. In addition, notice that the PROFIT field is empty, even though values appeared there in the original spreadsheet. This is because the spreadsheet calculated values for the profit column using a formula, subtracting the value in the cost column from the one in the sales column. If a profit value were required in the data file, you could insert it with the command

REPLACE ALL PROFIT WITH SALES – COST

Needless to say, data transfer to and from *dBase III Plus* usually requires a certain amount of fine-tuning of the information before it is in exactly the format you desire.

To write out information from a *dBase III Plus* file in a format that *Lotus 1-2-3* can understand, use the COPY TO command with the TYPE WKS option:

COPY TO <filename> TYPE WKS <conditions>

For example,

COPY TO PARTS TYPE WKS

creates a file named PARTS.WKS on the default drive which contains all of the records in the current data file. The new file can be read directly by *Lotus 1-2-3.*

COPY TO C:\LOTUS\DATA\MONTHLY TYPE WKS FOR MONTH = "JANUARY"

creates a *Lotus* worksheet file named MONTHLY in the LOTUS\DATA subdirectory on drive C. This new file contains only those records in which the field MONTH contains JANUARY.

Other Data-Transfer Options

dBase III Plus also allows you to share information with Software Publishing Corporation's popular *pfs:FILE* data-management program. The commands EXPORT and IMPORT can read and write *pfs:FILE* data files without having to convert to an intermediate format. In addition, the IMPORT command actually creates a new .DBF file from the information in the *pfs:FILE* data file; you do not have to CREATE a new *dBase* file prior to using the command.

The *pfs:FILE* program uses a user-designed screen format for displaying records. The *dBase III Plus* IMPORT command will convert these screens into *dBase* format (.FMT) files. In addition, the EXPORT command will send to *pfs:FILE* the format information found in the *dBase* .FMT file.

As an example, if you have a *pfs:FILE* data file called LEADS on the current drive and directory, the command

IMPORT FROM LEADS TYPE PFS

creates a *dBase* file called LEADS.DBF containing all the information from the *pfs:FILE* data file, and also a *dBase* format file called LEADS.FMT which closely follows the screen format used in the *pfs:FILE* file.

Other data-transfer options include *SYLK*-format files, which allow information to be passed between *dBase III Plus* and Microsoft's *Multiplan* spreadsheet, and *DIF* (Data Interchange Format) files which allow interchange with the *VisiCalc* spreadsheet program.

Almost every popular microcomputer program uses at least one of the file-transfer formats supported by *dBase III Plus,* so there is generally a way of sharing information among the programs.

If your data transfer needs are highly unusual, such as transferring information between computers that are incompatible both in terms of storage media and file format, you may need to explore the use of a commercial data-transfer and conversion service. These companies can handle tasks such as converting from open-reel magnetic tape to ASCII files on floppy disk, or from an outdated word processing system to more modern systems. Many companies offer these services, and their address and phone numbers can usually be found in the back pages of popular computer magazines.

Chapter 10
Error Messages

Chapter 10

Error Messages

Every *dBase III Plus* user encounters error messages now and then. Most are self-explanatory, but if you need more information, the *dBase III Plus* manual contains explanations of every message. A few error messages state the facts correctly, but do not always give the full picture. An error which seems to have a clear-cut cause may in fact be the symptom of quite another problem. The following list of error messages is not as inclusive as the list in the manual, but it contains some information that you will not find in the documentation provided with the program.

General Considerations

Sometimes you will receive error messages not relevant to the process at hand. If errors occur without apparent rhyme or reason, examine the CONFIG.SYS file in the root directory of the disk from which you boot DOS. The file should have the following lines in it for all machines over 256K (over 320K when using DOS versions 3.0 or higher):

FILES=20
BUFFERS=15

If the number of buffers is decreased, and especially if it is increased, many bizarre errors will occur. If you start experiencing errors in *dBase III Plus* after installing a new piece of software into your computer, you may want to check to see if the installation procedure for this new software changed the CONFIG.SYS file in some way. If so, put the FILE and BUFFER count back to the proper setting.

Other sources of errors which are hard to pin down are corrupted data files, and—more often—corrupted index files. The easiest way to find out whether an error is caused by index corruption is to try the offending command without an active index. If the problem goes away, suspect the index. In fact, suspect corrupted indices first for any problem. They are easy problems to test for, and easy problems to fix.

Data type mismatch. This error results from performing operations on dissimilar data types. For example, trying to place "01/04/87" into a date field will cause this error, since the quotes specify that the value is a string, not a date. The proper way to perform this operation would be to use the CTOD( ) (character-to-date) conversion function on the string. Strings can be converted to numbers and back with the VAL( ) and STR( ) functions. Perform a DISPLAY STRUCTURE to double-check which field types are used in your data file.

Disk full when writing <filename>. This error message is followed by a chance to delete old files. Be careful not to delete anything important; remove just enough old data or backup (.BAK) files to make room for the new file. Use DOS to do major housekeeping tasks.

End-of-file encountered. This error means you probably tried to SKIP when the record pointer was positioned at the last record in the file. If everything else looks okay and you still get this error, open the data file without any indices and try again. If the command which previously gave the error now works, suspect a corrupted index. Rebuild the index as needed.

File is not accessible. This error message sometimes occurs when creating or rebuilding an index file, even though the command you issue is correct. A bug in *dBase III* sometimes returns this message if the total length of the index filename plus the DOS pathname exceeds a certain length. For example,

```
INDEX ON LASTNAME TO
C:\DBASE\MAILLIST\LASTNAME.NDX
```

may cause an error message, while

```
INDEX ON LASTNAME TO LASTNAME
```

might work fine. Try some experiments if this error occurs for no apparent reason, and be sure to check the CONFIG.SYS file in the computer's root directory.

File too large, some data may be lost. The built-in word processor of *dBase III Plus* can only accommodate program (.PRG) files of about 4000 bytes—very small by most standards. This message appears if you attempt to use MODIFY COMMAND on a file that is larger than this—perhaps one that was created outside of *dBase*. If this happens, use the Esc key to end editing, and don't try to save the file. If you don't exit with the Esc key, the information will be lost for good.

If you work with larger files, or develop programs on a regular basis, you should use an external editor for creating program files. *dBase* allows you to specify the name of the editor in the CONFIG.DB file, and will activate it automatically whenever you type MODIFY COMMAND.

Index damaged. The contents of the index file may have been scrambled by shutting off the computer when a file was open, a disk failure, or any number of causes. In most cases, the REINDEX command will fix the problem, but you are better off rebuilding the index from scratch with the command INDEX ON <*expression*> TO <*filename*>.

Insufficient memory. You attempted to run an external program or issue a DOS command without sufficient RAM memory to handle the specified task.

Not a *dBase* database. This error is serious if the file you are trying to USE is clearly a *dBase III Plus* data file with a .DBF extension. This error message indicates that the file header is corrupted and the file cannot be read. This can result from a physical failure on the disk surface or from a data file which was not closed properly during its last use. Information in the file can be recovered with enough effort, but it requires a good deal of time and programming expertise.

Position is off the screen. This error results from attempting to display a field or variable onscreen at a row greater than 24 or a column greater than 79. If you write a program to list information onscreen by incrementing a row counter and issuing SAY commands to that row, be sure that the row cannot exceed 24.

Printer not ready. The printer connected to your computer is either off, off-line, out of paper, or connected to a printer port different from the one *dBase III Plus* is using.

Record is not in index. This error often occurs when using the BROWSE command. There are two common causes: a damaged index (see the discusson above of the *Index damaged* message) or an index based on an expression containing an STR( ) function in which a length is not specified. For example,

```
INDEX ON STR(CUST_NUM) TO CUSTOMER
```

builds an index that sorts the file properly but causes problems with BROWSE and certain other commands. STR( ) turns a number into a character string. If you convert a numeric field to a string, you must specify that the length of the string resulting from the function is the same as the length of the numeric field, including the decimal point. If you wanted to build an index on the five-digit field CUST_NUM, the proper way to do it is

INDEX ON STR(CUST_NUM,5) TO CUSTOMER

Record is out of range. Using the command GO 1000 while using a data file with less than 1000 records will give this error. However, the message can also result from a corrupted data file or index. If the record number is well within acceptable limits, try closing or rebuilding the index file.

Syntax error [in contents/column/group expression]. At the command level, *dBase* helps you spot a syntax error by placing a question mark above and to the right of the offending statement:

```
             ?
LOCATE FRO NAME = 'Smith'
```

A syntax error in a report column or mailing-label definition is harder to debug. MODIFY the report or label, and carefully check all of its contents.

Too many files are open. *dBase III Plus* allows up to 15 files to be open at any one time. A *file* can be a data file, an index, a format file, a program file, or any combination. If you get this error, issue the DISPLAY STATUS command to see what is going on. This will show the names of the data, index, and format files in use and help you see what may be causing the problem. Also, be sure that the CONFIG.SYS file in the root directory of the system drive contains the command FILES=20.

This error message occasionally appears when creating or debugging a complex program even though the maximum number of files has not been exceeded. If this occurs, QUIT *dBase* and reenter from the DOS prompt.

Chapter 11
Power-User Techniques

Chapter 11
Power-User Techniques

After working with *dBase III Plus* for a few weeks, you'll begin to flex your muscles and begin to push the program further. It won't be long before you're ready to try a few advanced operations, or even take the plunge into programming. Here are some tips for going forward.

Effective Hard-Disk Management

dBase III Plus users can increase the program's performance by properly organizing the way in which data and programs are stored on their hard disks. As with any applications program, *dBase III Plus* should reside in its own directory, separate from other programs. This improves the speed of the program and facilitates making regular backups.

You'll find it easier to manage your files if you also store all of the files related to a single *dBase* application (such as accounting, inventory, or mailing-list management) in a separate subdirectory below the directory in which *dBase III Plus* is stored. A typical hard-disk directory structure might look like this:

```
\ (root directory)
   \DBASE (dBase)
              \ACCOUNTS
              \MAILING
              \CLAIMS
              \CLIENTS
              \TRAVEL
   \WORD (word processor)
              \LETTERS
              \PERSONAL
              \FORMS
              \MISC
   \DOS    (DOS system files)
```

This arrangement allows you to group together all files related to one application (data, index, format, and program) in one directory for easy management.

To work with one of these applications, you would change to the proper directory with the DOS command CD:

CD \DBASE \CLIENTS

Next, you would use the DOS PATH command to select the directory in which your *dBase III Plus* program files are stored. This enables DOS to find the *dBase* program files even though you are currently logged into a different directory:

PATH = \DBASE

Next, run *dBase III Plus* by typing **dbase** at the DOS prompt. You will remain in the directory of your choice, and only the files in the current directory (in this example, \DBASE \CLIENTS) appear to the program.

Creating a DOS batch file can automate this process. A batch file like the one below will automatically change directories, run *dBase III Plus,* and return to the root (\) directory when finished:

```
ECHO OFF
CLS
PATH= \DBASE
CD \DBASE \CLIENTS
DBASE
ECHO OFF
CD \
CLS
DIR
```

Similar files could be created for each of the applications you manage with *dBase*. Then, you would merely have to type the name of the batch file at the DOS prompt and the application would be ready to use. See your DOS manual for more information about creating and using batch files.

Making Backups

The BACKUP command from DOS can be used to make archival copies of your program and data files to guard against loss from power interruptions or disk failure. If you use a directory structure like the one above, you can back up all of the files contained in the *dBase III Plus* directory as well as in directories below it with a single DOS command:

BACKUP C: \DBASE *.* A: /S

This command instructs DOS to back up onto drive A all of the files contained in the directory \DBASE on drive C, including any files found in subdirectories (/S). By making a small change to the command, you can back up only data (.DBF) files:

BACKUP C: \DBASE *.DBF A: /S

Exploring Programming

When you begin creating *dBase III Plus* programs, you'll realize just how powerful the program can be. Although you may not be ready to try any advanced programming techniques, a few simple programs can make many tasks much easier.

dBase III Plus programs consist of program (.PRG) files, and are created with the command MODIFY COMMAND <filename>. If a program file named <filename.PRG> exists, *dBase III Plus* will load and edit that file. If no file with the specified name currently exists, *dBase* will create one for you. The file can then be edited much like a document in a word processor. Pressing Ctrl-End saves the completed program to disk. When the program is completed and stored to disk, you can execute it from a DOS prompt by typing:

DO <filename>

where <filename> is the name you assigned to the program file.

A Simple Program

Suppose you use *dBase III Plus* to manage a mailing list. Without a program, you must manually enter all of the commands each time you need to add records, edit records, or produce labels. The following simple *dBase* program can automate these tasks, and control the application from an easy-to-read, customized menu:

```
** Displays menu and controls mailing-list management
DO WHILE .T.
    CLEAR
    @ 03,25 SAY "Mailing List Management"
    @ 04,25 SAY " * * * MAIN MENU * * *"
    @ 08,25 SAY "1) Add New Records"
    @ 10,25 SAY "2) Edit Existing Records"
    @ 12,25 SAY "3) Print Mailing Labels"
```

```
@ 14,25 SAY "Q) Quit dBase III Plus"
@ 20,0
   WAIT SPACE(25)+"What is your choice ? " TO CHOICE
   DO CASE
      CASE CHOICE = '1'
         USE PEOPLE
         SET FORMAT TO PEOPLE
         APPEND
         USE
      CASE CHOICE = '2'
         USE PEOPLE
         SET FORMAT TO PEOPLE
         EDIT
         USE
      CASE CHOICE = '3'
         USE PEOPLE
         LABEL FORM PEOPLE TO PRINT SAMPLE
         USE
      CASE UPPER(CHOICE) = 'Q'
         QUIT
   ENDCASE
ENDDO
```

This program may look complex at first, but it is basically a collection of *dBase III Plus* commands, much like they would be entered from the dot prompt. Only two of the commands in this program—DO WHILE and DO CASE—are unique to programming and are not used directly from the dot prompt. Let's examine the program section-by-section and see what it does.

The first line is a comment, ignored by *dBase* since it begins with asterisks (*). Comment lines are used to record notes about the program, such as the date it was created, the author, and the purpose of the program. Good programmers make liberal use of comments in their work.

Next, a loop is established. The command DO WHILE and the corresponding ENDDO at the end of the program mark an area that is to be performed again and again until a specified condition is met. In this example, no condition is specified (DO WHILE .T. simply means keep executing the loop until stopped by some other command), so you must provide a way of breaking out of the loop. Within the DO WHILE loop, a series of commands clears the screen and displays a menu of user options.

Next, the cursor is moved to line 20 (with the @ 20,0 command), and input is requested from the user with the WAIT command. WAIT displays a prompt, and the program waits for the user to press a key. The value of the key pressed is then recorded in a memory variable (in this case, a variable called CHOICE).

After the user presses a key, the selection must be evaluated and appropriate action taken. The DO CASE command allows us to take different action based on the value of CHOICE. For example, if the user pressed the 1 key, the command CASE CHOICE = '1' will perform the actions listed (USE the data file, open the format file, append records, and close the file). Likewise, if the user pressed the 2 key in response to the prompt, the program opens the data file for editing. If the 3 key is pressed, mailing labels are produced. To quit the program (and exit *dBase*) the user would press the Q key.

Note the command CASE UPPER(CHOICE) = 'Q'. This converts the user's input to uppercase before comparing it to *Q* so that it will work even if the user enters a lowercase *q*. A well-designed program makes allowances for inexact user input. Following the ENDCASE command, which marks the end of the DO CASE section, there is an ENDDO command, which marks the end of the loop created with DO WHILE. When the program reaches this point, it will loop back to the start of the DO loop and begin again. Only by pressing the Q key can the user break out of the loop and exit the program.

Learning More

Although advanced programming is beyond the scope of this book, there are a number of publications available on advanced *dBase III Plus* techniques and programming. One excellent source of information for *dBase III Plus* users is *Data Based Advisor* magazine, which is aimed specifically at database users. Each issue contains articles that will appeal to both the novice and the seasoned *dBase* user.

Another invaluable source of information and help are the many database user's groups affiliated with computer clubs and professional organizations. The Boston Computer Society is an example of a diverse group of users who can often help with the design and use of database systems.

Chapter 12

Customizing *dBase III Plus*

Chapter 12

Customizing *dBase III Plus*

Part of the power of *dBase III Plus* comes from its flexibility. You can configure *dBase III Plus* to respond to commands as you wish.

The CONFIG.DB File

When *dBase III Plus* first loads, it looks for a file called CONFIG.DB in the current directory. This file contains a set of operating conditions that establish how *dBase* will respond to commands. The default CONFIG.DB file, created when *dBase* is installed, contains the following information:

STATUS=ON
COMMAND=ASSIST

This tells *dBase* to put the status bar at the bottom of the screen, and to automatically enter the *dBase* Assistant mode. This is fine for the first-time user, but it won't be long before you are ready to configure *dBase* your own way.

To modify CONFIG.DB, first load it into the *dBase* word processor with the command

MODIFY COMMAND CONFIG.DB

Once the file is loaded, you can edit it and save it with Ctrl-W as you would any other program file. However, changes made to the file will not take effect until *dBase* is next started up from DOS. CONFIG.DB is only read during the startup process.

Almost all of the environmental (SET) commands can be executed by CONFIG.DB, although they are entered in the file in a different way than they are at the dot prompt. For example, the SET TALK OFF command would be entered in the CONFIG.DB file as

TALK = OFF

rather than as SET TALK OFF as you would from the dot prompt.

Chapter 5 gives a complete listing of environmental commands along with their default (startup) settings.

Commands other than environmental (SET) commands can be executed from CONFIG.DB by preceding them with COMMAND =. For example, to get a directory of data files upon startup, include this command in CONFIG.DB:

COMMAND = DIR

CONFIG.DB allows you to program nine of the ten function keys on your keyboard. (The F1 function key is always reserved for help.) For example, to program function key F9 so that it enters the command CLOSE DATABASES whenever it is pressed, you would place the following line in the CONFIG.DB file:

F9 = "CLOSE DATABASES;"

The semicolon at the end of the command instructs *dBase III Plus* to include a carriage-return (Enter) character as well.

You can use CONFIG.DB to call a text editor other than the built-in *dBase* editor to use when the MODIFY COMMAND command is issued. In this way, you can create and modify program and format files using a text editor or word processor of your own choosing. To specify a particular text editor or word processor, include a line of the form

TEDIT = <filename>

where <filename> is the name of your word processor file. For example, to specify *WordStar* as your text editor, include this line in CONFIG.DB:

TEDIT = WS.COM

You can also specify another word processor for editing memo fields in a similar fashion by using

WP = <filename>

where <filename> is the name of your word processor file. For example, to use *WordStar* for this function as well, you would include the line

WP = WS.COM

It is even possible to change the *dBase III Plus* dot prompt into something a bit friendlier. Include in the CONFIG.DB file a line of the form:

PROMPT = <new prompt message>

For example, you might use

PROMPT = What Next?

Other configuration settings such as BUCKET, MVARSIZ, and GETS are less frequently changed, and apply primarily to programmers and applications developers.

The CONFIG.DB file that I am most comfortable with is as follows:

CONFIRM = ON
BELL = OFF
HELP = OFF
TEDIT = \DBASE\NE.COM
COMMAND = CLEAR

This file sets the operating parameters the way I like, and specifies my favorite text editor—the Norton Editor (NE.COM)—for programming and format design. It then clears the screen prior to my issuing any command.

Experiment with the different commands and environmental settings until you find those which suit you best and design your own CONFIG.DB file accordingly.

Chapter 13

dBase III Plus in Action

Chapter 13

dBase III Plus in Action

Learning commands and what they do is one thing, but to know how these can be put into action in the real world is another. *dBase* is at work in millions of businesses worldwide. This chapter provides two examples of rather typical applications of *dBase* programming. The first shows how a membership database for a hypothetical museum works. What is presented here can provide a framework for similar applications in *your* real world: perhaps a club or church membership list. The second application is an inventory database. Many businesses need to keep inventories, and while the business which the illustration uses to make its point is more mythical than typical, the inventory system it uses is real. It can be easily modified to suit many inventory applications in the business world.

A Membership Database

The New England Toaster Museum maintains one of the finest exhibits of small kitchen appliances in the country, but its limited budget makes expansion and improvements difficult. The museum membership consists of those few toaster and toaster-oven fanciers who are willing to contribute whatever they can to keep the museum at the forefront of breakfast-preparation technology. A limited number of fund-raising events, such as the annual Waffle Breakfast and the always-popular Blender Night, bring in some extra income, but keeping in touch with members and past attendees proved too difficult for the mostly volunteer staff to manage by hand.

After a generous member contributed a personal computer and a copy of *dBase III Plus*, the museum's director decided to place the membership list on the computer. The staff hoped that this would make it easier to produce mailing labels and form letters, and would help keep track of contributions received from members and contributors.

The first stage of the project is to design a file to hold name-and-address information on the members. Since most mailing labels are 3½ inches in width, a 10-character-per-inch printer can fit 35 characters on a single line. Excessively long fields in the data file (such as a 50-character address field) are wasteful. The file design which works best is

Field	Field Name	Type	Width	Dec
1	LASTNAME	Character	15	
2	FIRSTNAME	Character	15	
3	MIDDLE	Character	1	
4	TITLE	Character	4	
5	COMPANY	Character	35	
6	ADDRESS	Character	35	
7	ADDRESS2	Character	35	
8	CITY	Character	25	
9	STATE	Character	2	
10	ZIP	Character	5	
11	PHONE	Character	14	
12	MEMB_NO	Character	6	
13	MEMB_TYPE	Character	4	
14	RENEWAL	Date	8	

To make data entry and retrieval easier, the museum uses a format file made with the CREATE SCREEN command. The format file organizes the screen into an easy-to-read form during all full-screen operations:

Figure 13-1. A Sample Screen for Data Entry

New England Toaster Museum
Mailing/Membership List

Member Number: ________

Name Last: ____________ **First:** __________ **MI:** ____ **Title:** ______

Company: ______________________________

Address: ______________________________

____

City: ____________________ **State:** ______ **ZIP:** ______

Phone: (____) ______

Member Type: ______ **Renewal Date:** ___/___/___

The main data file, MEMBERS.DBF, holds names and addresses of the 1500 dues-paying members of the museum, as well as names of the more than 5000 toaster-fanciers who have visited the museum in the past. The MEMB_TYPE (member-type) field is used to identify those people who are paying members; an *M* is placed in this field for those who are members. The RENEWAL field holds the date that the person's membership is due for renewal.

Mailing Labels

The museum produces a monthly newsletter describing new advances in kitchen-appliance technology. The formerly time-consuming task of hand addressing all of the envelopes is simplified by using *dBase III Plus* to produce mailing labels. The label design (stored in a file called MAILING.LBL) is very simple:

```
1  TITLE,FIRSTNAME,MIDDLE,LASTNAME
2  COMPANY
3  ADDRESS
4  ADDRESS2
5  TRIM(CITY) | "," | STATE,ZIP
```

Since *dBase* automatically removes blank lines from the finished label, the COMPANY and ADDRESS2 fields will not appear when they are empty. A finished label looks like this:

Mr. Robert Dayton
Northern Electric Products, Inc.
1247 Eastern Blvd.
Saugerties, NY 10528

Since it is a nonprofit organization, the museum qualifies for special postal rates. In order for the post office to accept mail at this rate, however, the mailing must be sorted by zip code. To accomplish this, it's easy to build a temporary index to organize the file in the desired way:

```
USE MEMBERS
INDEX ON ZIP TO ZIP
```

The labels can then be produced in this order by entering

```
LABEL FORM MAILING TO PRINT SAMPLE
```

At several times during the year, the museum conducts membership drives inviting prior visitors to become contributing members. This mailing is directed at previous visitors, but it is not intended to go to those people who are already members. Since current members are identified by an *M* in the

MEMB_TYPE field, the labels need to be produced for all records which do *not* have an *M* in this field:

LABEL FORM MAILING TO PRINT FOR .NOT. "M" $ MEMB_TYPE SAMPLE

This command directs *dBase III Plus* to produce labels for all records in which an *M* is not (*.NOT.*) contained within the field MEMB_TYPE. (The $ character means *contained within.*)

Since we use the $ operator, the position of this character within the field is not important, and other identifying codes can be placed in the same field without causing confusion. The museum places a *B* in the MEMB_TYPE field for those members who are on the board of directors, an *A* is used to identify members of the Appliance Committee, and so on. Some very active members have three or four different codes in their record. This makes it possible to direct mailings to one or more subgroups at the same time. For example, to send a mailing to members who are either on the Appliance Committee (*A*) or are Coffee Maker fans (*C*), the command is

LABEL FORM MAILING TO PRINT FOR "A" $ MEM_TYPE .OR. "C" $ MEM_TYPE SAMPLE

Another regular mailing is the monthly renewal notice, which is directed at members whose membership is due for renewal in the upcoming month. This requires a test on the month portion of the RENEWAL field, which can be accessed with the MONTH( ) function. For example, to send a notice to all members who are up for renewal during the month of June, the command is

LABEL FORM MAILING TO PRINT FOR MONTH(RENEWAL) = 6 SAMPLE

Notice that the 6 is not in quotes. Since the MONTH( ) function returns a numeric value, the value being compared to it can be entered directly, without the quotes.

Membership Cards

By creating a label-format file which aligns the information properly, the museum is able to use *dBase III Plus* to print membership wallet cards for the members. Almost any business-form supply company can provide preprinted cards mounted on tractor-feed stock. As far as *dBase* is concerned, the steps involved in printing these cards is the same as for producing mailing labels. The only difference is the fact that a separate label-format file must be used for the job. The format used for cards must have the proper spacing between cards, and the proper alignment of *dBase* fields with the information which is already printed on the card.

Tracking Gifts and Donations

During the course of a year, members send money to help support the museum. These payments may be dues or just gifts. To keep track of which members have contributed and how much they have sent, the museum needs a second file, called CONTRIB.DBF. This file records the amount of each contribution or gift received, the date it was received, the amount, a code identifying the type of contribution (gift, dues, and so on), and the membership number of the person making the contribution. This eliminates redundant information, since the membership number can be used to establish a relation between this and the main membership file. The file structure of CONTRIB.DBF is

Field	Field Name	Type	Width	Dec
1	MEMB_NO	Character	6	
2	GIFT_DATE	Date	8	
3	GIFT_AMT	Numeric	7	2
4	GIFT_TYPE	Character	1	

With this arrangement, one member can make any number of contributions, with each recorded separately. A minimum amount of storage space is used for each record, yet all of the information you could want is still available. If you wanted to see how much has been contributed by member 1004, list the contribution file and view all of the records separately:

USE CONTRIB
LIST OFF FOR MEMB_NO = "1004"

```
MEMB_NO   GIFT_DATE   GIFT_AMT   GIFT_TYPE

1004      11/17/86    100.00         D
1004      01/04/87     25.00         R
1004      03/28/87     10.00         P
```

or simply ask for the total amount contributed by this member:

```
USE CONTRIB
SUM GIFT_AMT FOR MEMB_NO = "1004"
```

```
3 Records summed
GIFT_AMT
  135.00
```

The GIFT_DATE or GIFT_TYPE fields can be used to limit the selection of records to those which match specified conditions. For example, to see how much was received for renewals (gift type R) during 1987, enter

```
SUM GIFT_AMT FOR GIFT_TYPE = "R" .AND. YEAR
   (GIFT_DATE) = 1987
```

```
1450 Records summed
GIFT_AMT
  57890.00
```

Linking this file to the member file allows the museum to send mailings or produce lists based on information found in the contribution file. For example, the museum wanted to call a select group of members to invite them to a fund-raising dinner. The only members that were to be invited were those who have contributed more than $100 at any one time during 1986. To do this, it is necessary to establish a relation between the two files:

```
SELECT 1
USE MEMBERS INDEX MEMB_NO
SELECT 2
USE CONTRIB
SET RELATION TO MEMB_NO INTO MEMBERS
```

With the two files linked in this way, each time the record pointer in the contribution file (CONTRIB) is moved, the record pointer in the member file (MEMBERS) will be positioned at the appropriate record. It is then easy to produce a list of members meeting the specified condition:

```
LIST MEMBERS->LASTNAME,MEMBERS->FIRSTNAME,
   MEMBERS->PHONE FOR GIFT_AMT >= 100 .AND. YEAR
   (GIFT_DATE) = 1986
```

Tracking Events

A second subfile is established to record attendance at the fund-raising events and social functions that the museum sponsors. This file helps the museum directors see which events are the most popular, and also to keep in touch with members who have attended events in the past. Like the contribution file, the event file uses the membership number to provide a link to the membership file. The file structure chosen for the event file is

Field	Field Name	Type	Width	Dec
1	MEMB_NO	Character	6	
2	EVENT_DATE	Date	8	
3	EVENT_NAME	Character	35	

Each time a member attends a fund-raising event, a record is added to the EVENT file, and the member number, date of the event, and a description of the event is recorded. This allows the museum staff to see who attended a given event or to see which events a given member has attended. For example, to get a list of the names of people who attended the annual Garbage Disposal Jamboree, the following commands would do the job:

```
SELECT 1
USE MEMBERS INDEX MEMB_NO
SELECT 2
USE EVENTS
SET RELATION TO MEMB_NO INTO MEMBERS
LIST MEMBERS->FIRSTNAME,MEMBERS->LASTNAME
  FOR EVENT_NAME = "Garbage Disposal Jamboree"
```

To see which events member 1445 has attended, enter

```
LIST EVENT_DATE,EVENT_NAME FOR MEMB_NO = "1445"
```

EVENT_DATE	EVENT_NAME
01/04/86	Coffee Filter Dance
06/30/86	Fondue Picnic
09/25/86	Waffle & Steam Iron Breakfast

Expanding the System

These three simple files provide a great deal of information about the museum, and make managing the facility a great deal easier than it was when a manual system was in place. The museum staff has some future plans for the system that they hope to incorporate soon. Each feature they plan to add is easily within the scope of *dBase III Plus*.

Programmed operation. Not every member of the museum staff has the computer skills required to use *dBase III Plus* from the dot prompt. One of the first enhancements that the museum plans is to design a menu-driven interface for users of the system. The planned menu will provide all of the major system functions and will look something like this:

New England Toaster Museum

MAIN MENU

1) Enter/Edit Member Records
2) Enter/Edit Contribution Records
3) Enter/Edit Event Records
4) Print Mailing Labels
5) Produce Reports
Q) Quit

What is your Selection?

This way, even someone with little or no knowledge of *dBase III Plus* commands can still use the system for most daily functions.

Pledge management. Many members prefer to contribute a small amount at a time and pledge to give a certain amount each month. The staff hopes to add a file which records these pledges so that they can send out reminders when they are due.

Expenditure tracking. A nonprofit organization has unique accounting needs, and *dBase III Plus* has the flexibility to provide a complete method of tracking both income and expenditures.

Exhibit inventory. Eventually, the staff hopes to keep exhibit records on *dBase III Plus*, allowing them to see which appliances are on display, which are in storage, and which are on loan to (or from) other appliance museums.

An Inventory Database

The Acme Supply Corporation is one of the West's largest suppliers of mail-order supplies for cartoon characters. If you need a pair of rocket-powered roller skates or a high-speed avalanche maker on short notice, no other supplier can be relied on to deliver the goods like Acme.

Naturally, managing the inventory of a company which sells items as diverse as magnetic bird seed and 75-foot slingshots is a challenge, to say the least. Acme must keep a large number of items in stock. It must know what each item is, how many are available for sale, and when and where to reorder supplies. That way, its customers can get the immediate service from Acme which they have come to expect. Items will be ready for immediate delivery. This is just the sort of system that *dBase* is designed to handle.

Over the years, Acme has developed an item-coding system that has proved very efficient. Each item is assigned a six-character code of letters and numbers. The first two characters identify the type of item (BS for birdseed, RO for rockets, and so on).The last four characters are numbers used for a more specific item description. This design makes it easy to incorporate the Acme inventory into a *dBase* data file. This file, ITEMS.DBF, has inventory records for the thousands of items regularly stocked by Acme. A small section of the file is shown below:

ITEM_NO	TYPE	DESCRIP	COUNT	MIN	MAX	COST
BS2000	BIRDSEED	MAGNETIC 100LB. BAG	45	20	100	29.95
BA4250	BAZOOKA	STRAIGHT-JACKET EJECTING	12	4	15	78.00
PE7500	PELLETS	INSTANT EARTHQUAKE	250	200	275	.75
PE9725	PELLETS	DEHYDRATED ROCKS	125	75	150	2.00
SS3789	SHOES	SPRING POWERED	12	15	20	17.50
CO1500	COSTUME	FEMALE TAZMANIAN DEVIL	5	6	10	24.00
TN1000	TNT	SINGLE STICK	575	300	600	1.00
RO1000	ROCKET	FULL SIZE - SINGLE SEAT	6	3	8	965.00

Each record holds the item number (ITEM_NO), the item type (TYPE), and a brief description (DESCRIP). In addition, the quantity on hand of each item is recorded in the COUNT field, the minimum number desired is recorded in the MIN field, and the maximum number desired is held in the MAX field. Each item's cost is stored in the COST field.

Although the file is very large (over 15,000 records), creating an index on the ITEM_NO field makes it possible to locate individual records quickly once the item number is known:

USE ITEMS
INDEX ON ITEM_NO TO ITEMNO (Do only once)

FIND TN1000
Record = 7856

Locating records by information other than the item number is possible, but not as fast. For example, a frustrated customer may call Acme to inquire what items are available to help him deal with a plague of pesky cockroaches. He may have already decided that explosives are the only logical choice, and wants to know what is available in the way of things that go boom in the night. Acme sells several choices of TNT and many other exploding items. To get a listing of both TNT and any other items which explode, the Acme sales representative enters:

LIST FOR TYPE = "TNT" .OR. "EXPLODING" $ DESCRIP

and gets the following list:

ITEM_NO	TYPE	DESCRIP	COUNT	MIN	MAX	COST
BS5000	BIRDSEED	EXPLODING - 100LB. BAG	5	5	10	29.95
TN1000	TNT	SINGLE STICK	575	300	600	1.00
TN2000	TNT	FULL CASE	10	10	15	36.00
ED1250	DART	THREE-FIN - EXPLODING	100	75	150	7.00
EC4500	CIGAR	EXPLODING - LOW POWER	12	10	15	3.00
EC5500	CIGAR	EXPLODING - MEDIUM POWER	23	25	50	5.00
EC6500	CIGAR	EXPLODING - HIGH POWER	45	50	60	7.00
EC7500	CIGAR	EXPLODING - NUCLEAR	15	12	15	269.00

This command lists any records which contain TNT in the TYPE field or the character string EXPLODING in the description field (DESCRIP).

Handling Inventory Levels

Acme's inventory-management system assigns each product a minimum count in the MIN field. When the number on hand of a given product falls below this amount, it is time to reorder the product from the manufacturer. Each item is also assigned a desired maximum inventory level in the MAX field. This indicates the largest number that should be on hand at any one time. This assures that the item will be not be overstocked.

You can tell which items are in short supply by listing those records in which the value held in COUNT is equal to or less than the value in MIN. At the same time, you can also see how many of the items need to be ordered, since the order quantity is always the desired inventory level (in MAX) minus the number already on hand (in COUNT). The following command shows which items are needed, and the number which should be ordered:

LIST ITEM_NO,TYPE,DESCRIP,COUNT,MAX − COUNT FOR COUNT <= MIN

ITEM_NO	TYPE	DESCRIP	COUNT	MAX − COUNT
BS5000	BIRDSEED	EXPLODING - 100LB. BAG	5	5
SS3789	SHOES	SPRING POWERED	12	8
CO1200	COSTUME	FEMALE ROAD-RUNNER	2	2
CO1500	COSTUME	FEMALE TAZMANIAN DEVIL	5	5
PE8500	PELLETS	DEHYDRATED BOULDERS	100	100
TN2000	TNT	FULL CASE	10	5

RO2000	ROCKET	BACKPACK MODEL	12	8
RO3000	ROCKET	SLED W/ TRACK	3	2
BB3000	BALL	BOWLING - 30LB.	5	7
SK1500	SKATE	ROLLER - STANDARD	7	5
EC5500	CIGAR	EXPLODING - MEDIUM POWER	23	27
EC6500	CIGAR	EXPLODING - HIGH POWER	45	15
PT4568	PAINT	TWO-LANE ROAD: LEFT TURN	1	4
VH5001	VEHICLE	UNICYCLE	25	11

This LIST command includes four database fields and a derived value, MAX – COUNT. This number shows the required order quantity.

Values derived from database fields also allow the Acme staff to produce price sheets from the inventory files. Because the data file contains cost figures, retail prices can be derived by multiplying the cost by a markup value. Acme marks most items up by 50 percent, which means the formula COST * 1.5 will display an item's selling price.

If someone is planning some undercover work, and needs a price list of the various costumes that Acme sells, the following command will provide the list they need:

SET HEADING OFF (Suppress field names)
LIST OFF ITEM_NO, TYPE, DESCRIP, COST * 1.5 FOR TYPE ="COSTUME"

CO1200	COSTUME	FEMALE ROAD-RUNNER	67.50
CO1500	COSTUME	FEMALE TAZMANIAN DEVIL	36.00
CO1650	COSTUME	SUPER HERO - CAPE & COWL	75.00
CO1655	COSTUME	SUPER HERO - SUIT & BOOT	150.00

If the customer needs a copy of this list, adding TO PRINT to the end of above command sends the list to the printer.

Format Screens

The Acme inventory system is accessed by several different departments, which include the warehouse staff, salespeople, and management. However, Acme wants its cost figures to remain confidential and does not wish the warehouse staff to be able to access costs. At the same time, salespeople need access to both inventory levels and cost figures, while they do not need to know minimum and maximum stock levels. To provide each department with the information it needs while keeping confidential data out of sight, Acme designed several different format screens, one for each department.

When the sales department uses the system, they issue the command SET FORMAT TO SALES, which activates the format file SALES.FMT. This file contains SAYs and GETs for all fields in the file, except for MIN and MAX. Another format file, WAREHOUS.FMT, contains the MIN and MAX fields but omits the COST field. A third format file, MANAGE.FMT, contains all fields in the file for use by management only.

Tracking Vendors

Acme purchases their products from a number of different vendors, and producing purchase orders is a time-consuming task. Recently, the system was enhanced by adding a new field to the main inventory file, ITEMS.DBF. This eight-character field, VENDOR, holds a code identifying the vendor from whom the item is purchased. A second data file, called VENDORS.DBF contains more detailed information about each vendor, including an address, terms, and ordering policies:

Field	Field Name	Type	Width	Dec
1	VEND_CODE	Character	8	
2	NAME	Character	30	
3	ADDRESS	Character	30	
4	CITY	Character	25	
5	STATE	Character	2	
6	ZIP	Character	5	
7	PHONE	Character	14	
8	CONTACT	Character	30	
9	TERMS	Character	10	
10	MIN_ORDER	Numeric	6	2

Now, you can produce a purchase order for each vendor by including the vendor code in the LIST command. For example, list which items need to be ordered from Federal Products Company (vendor code FEDCO), enter

```
LIST OFF ITEM_NO,TYPE,DESCRIP,COUNT,MAX – COUNT
   FOR COUNT <= MIN .AND. VENDOR = "FEDCO"
```

The name, address and other information for that particular vendor can then be retrieved from the VENDOR.DBF file:

```
USE VENDOR
INDEX ON VEND_CODE TO VENDOR
FIND FEDCO
```

Managing Customers

Although some customers order from Acme only once, many others call Acme regularly. Acme decided to add a customer file to its *dBase* system for those customers. With a customer file, Acme is able to make ordering easier for the customer, and it can stay in touch with customers by using direct-mail advertising.

Field	Field Name	Type	Width	Dec
1	NAME	Character	30	
2	ADDRESS	Character	30	
3	CITY	Character	20	
4	STATE	Character	2	
5	ZIP	Character	5	
6	PHONE	Character	14	
7	TERMS	Character	10	
8	LAST_ORDER	Date	8	
9	YTD_PURCH	Numeric	7	2

Acme needed to develop a system which assigned a unique identifying code to each customer, since many of their customers have the same name. To solve this problem, Acme used the customer's daytime telephone number (area code and number) as the index key field of the customer file. An index was built accordingly:

INDEX ON PHONE TO CUSTOMER

If a customer has ordered from Acme in the past, the customer can simply give his or her phone number to the salesperson, who then performs a FIND using the phone number. If a customer record exists, the rest of the information (name, address, method of payment, and so on) can then be retrieved from the customer file. This saves hours of work on the phone.

Expanding the System Further

With inventory and customer information available from the computer, Acme has the basic components of an order-entry system already in place. In fact, by creating an invoice file and an invoice-detail file like those described in chapter 7, the system is almost complete. The invoice number is used to link records from the invoice-detail file with records in the invoice file. Each invoice consists of a single record in the invoice file, and as many records in the invoice-detail file as there are items on the invoice. This allows the system to use as many records as necessary to process an invoice which has a large number of items, yet does not waste space on those invoices which consist of only one or two items.

An invoice file would need to contain the following information:

Customer code (phone number)
Date ordered
Invoice number
Date shipped
Invoice total

The items sold on each invoice would be recorded separately, in an invoice-detail file:

Invoice Number
Item Number
Quantity
Price

Since many of their customers are notoriously slow in paying, Acme sells most of their products on a COD or prepaid basis. Still, the order-entry system can be expanded into a full-fledged accounts-receivable system by adding a few modifications. This would allow Acme to send statements and bills to their charge customers, apply payments to open invoices, and handle credits and returns.

Further Still

Material management. Some of Acme's products are not purchased in a ready-to-sell form, and must be assembled from various parts. For example, the popular Desert Ski Kit consists of a pair of skis, a back-mounted refrigerator, a high-speed ice maker, and a large electric fan. If one part of the package is out of stock, the kit cannot be sold. By setting up a subfile with the package name as its key field and with other fields containing the necessary parts, Acme can make sure that the entire package is in stock.

Sales tracking. Each outside salesperson at Acme is assigned monthly sales goals based on past performance. If a salesperson's performance falls off, management needs to know. By recording sales figures in *dBase* files, the Acme staff would be able to spot trends by salesperson, territory, and time of year.

General accounting. Accounting functions such as general ledger, accounts payable, and payroll are often performed with *dBase III Plus*. Although it is possible to program *dBase* to handle these functions on your own, many ready-to-run accounting systems are available which are written in the *dBase* programming language. Since these packages are already designed and debugged, they are a cost-effective way of approaching the task. If any needed features are not present in the original package, they can usually be added with little effort.

Appendices

Appendix A

For More Information

Anderson, Dick, Cynthia Cooper, and Bill Demsey. 1986. *dBase III Tips & Traps.* Berkeley, CA: McGraw-Hill.

Dinerstein, Nelson T. 1985. *dBase III for the Programmer.* Glenview, IL: Scott, Foresman and Company.

Hergert, Douglas. 1985. *dBase III: The Microsoft Desktop Dictionary and Cross-Reference Guide.* Bellevue, WA: Microsoft Press.

Prague, Cary N., and James E. Hammitt. 1986. *The dBase III Programming Handbook.* Bluc Ridgc Summit, PA: TAB Books.

Appendix B

Quick-Reference Command Summary

?

Syntax: ? <expression>

Use: Shows the current value of <expression>.

@

Syntax: @ <*row,col*> SAY <expression>
@ <*row,col*> GET <fieldname/memory variable>

Use: @...SAY displays text and data at specified locations on the screen or printer. @...GET allows user entry into data fields or memory variables.

@...TO

Syntax: @ <*row1,col1*> [CLEAR] TO <*row2,col2*> [DOUBLE]

Use: Draws single- or double-line boxes, or clears specified portions of the screen.

APPEND

Syntax: APPEND [BLANK]

Use: Starts a full-screen editing mode in which new records can be added to the currently active database file. APPEND BLANK adds a single blank record to the end of the file, but does not start the editing mode.

APPEND FROM

Syntax: APPEND FROM <filename> [FOR <condition>] [TYPE <type>]

Use: Adds records to the currently active database file from the database file specified by <filename>.

AVERAGE

Syntax: AVERAGE <field(s)> [WHILE <condition>] [FOR <condition>] [TO <memory variable(s)>]

Use: Calculates the numeric average of the specified fields.

BROWSE

Syntax: BROWSE [FIELDS <field(s)>]

Use: Starts a full-screen editing and scanning mode in which as many as 19 records can be viewed on the screen at once.

CLEAR

Syntax: CLEAR

Use: Clears the display screen.

CLEAR ALL

Syntax: CLEAR ALL

Use: Closes all open database files and their associated index, format, and memo files.

CLEAR MEMORY

Syntax: CLEAR MEMORY

Use: Releases all currently active memory variables.

CLOSE

Syntax: CLOSE <filetype> / ALL

Use: Closes all open files, or all files of a specified type. Memory variables are not affected.

CONTINUE

Syntax: CONTINUE

Use: Resumes the search for records specified by a LOCATE command.

COPY

Syntax: COPY TO <filename> [FIELDS <field(s)>] [FOR <condition>] [TYPE <type>]

Use: Copies all or part of the database file currently in use to a new database file.

COPY FILE

Syntax: COPY FILE <filename1> TO <filename2> [FOR <condition>] [TYPE <type>]

Use: Makes a duplicate of the file specified as <filename1> with the name specified in <filename2>.

COPY STRUCTURE

Syntax: COPY STRUCTURE TO <filename> [FIELDS <field(s)>]

Use: Creates a new, empty database file with the same structure as the file currently in use.

COUNT

Syntax: COUNT [<condition>] [WHILE <condition>] [FOR <condition>] [TO <memory variable>]

Use: Counts the number of records matching the specified condition in the database file currently in use.

CREATE

Syntax: CREATE <filename>

Use: Creates a new *dBase III Plus* database file.

CREATE LABEL

Syntax: CREATE LABEL <filename>

Use: Starts a full-screen editing mode which allows the design of a new label-format (.LBL) file.

CREATE REPORT

Syntax: CREATE REPORT <filename>

Use: Starts a full-screen editing mode which allows the design of a new report-format (.FRM) file.

CREATE SCREEN

Syntax: CREATE SCREEN <filename>

Use: Starts a full-screen editing mode which allows the design of a new screen format (.FMT) file.

DELETE

Syntax: DELETE [WHILE <condition>] [FOR <condition>]

Use: Marks one or more records for deletion from the database file.

DIR

Syntax: DIR [<skeleton>]

Use: Displays a listing of the database files (.DBF) on the current disk drive, along with information about the files.

DISPLAY

Syntax: DISPLAY [[FIELDS] <fields>] [WHILE <condition>] [FOR <condition>] [TO PRINT]

Use: Shows the contents of a record or series of records.

DISPLAY HISTORY

Syntax: DISPLAY HISTORY

Use: Shows the most recent series of commands typed at the dot prompt.

DISPLAY MEMORY

Syntax: DISPLAY MEMORY [TO PRINT]

Use: Shows the currently active memory variables along with their type, size, and status.

DISPLAY STATUS

Syntax: DISPLAY STATUS [TO PRINT]

Use: Shows the status of the current operating session.

DISPLAY STRUCTURE

Syntax: DISPLAY STRUCTURE [TO PRINT]

Use: Shows the field names, type, and size for the records of the currently active database file.

EDIT

Syntax: EDIT [FIELDS <field list>] [WHILE <condition>] [FOR <condition>]

Use: Starts a full-screen editing mode in which the contents of a record can be changed as needed.

EJECT

Syntax: EJECT

Use: Issues a form-feed command to the printer.

ERASE

Syntax: ERASE <filename.extension>

Use: Deletes the specified file from disk.

FIND

Syntax: FIND <character string> / <n>

Use: Locates a character string or numeric value in the indexed field of the active database file.

GO/GOTO

Syntax: GO <n>/TOP/BOTTOM
GOTO <n>/TOP/BOTTOM

Use: Positions the record pointer to the record number specified by <n>. GO TOP and GO BOTTOM move the record pointer to the first or last records in the database file, respectively.

HELP

Syntax: HELP [<keyword>]

Use: Displays a menu of help topics on the screen.

INDEX

Syntax: INDEX ON <key> TO <filename>

Use: Creates an index (.NDX) file which controls the order of the current database file.

LABEL FORM

Syntax: LABEL FORM <filename> [WHILE <condition>] [FOR <condition>] [TO PRINT] [SAMPLE]

Use: Activates a label-format file previously created with the CREATE LABEL or MODIFY LABEL commands.

LIST

Syntax: LIST [<field list>] [WHILE <condition>] [FOR <condition>] [TO PRINT]

Use: Displays the contents of the database file to screen or printer.

LOCATE

Syntax: LOCATE [WHILE <condition>] [FOR <condition>]

Use: Searches the current database file for the first record which matches the specified condition.

MODIFY LABEL

Syntax: MODIFY LABEL <filename>

Use: Allows modification an existing label-format (.LBL) file.

MODIFY REPORT

Syntax: MODIFY REPORT <filename>

Use: Allows modification of an existing report-format (.FRM) file.

MODIFY SCREEN

Syntax: MODIFY SCREEN <filename>

Use: Allows modification of an existing format (.FMT) file.

MODIFY STRUCTURE

Syntax: MODIFY STRUCTURE

Use: Allows changes to the structure of the current database file. New fields can be added, and existing fields can be modified or deleted altogether.

PACK

Syntax: PACK

Use: Removes records from the active database file that have been marked for deletion with the DELETE command.

QUIT

Syntax: QUIT

Use: Closes all open database files and indices and exits *dBase III Plus*.

READ

Syntax: READ [SAVE]

Use: Causes *dBase III Plus* to ask for data through @...GET commands.

RECALL

Syntax: RECALL ALL / [WHILE <condition>] [FOR <condition>]

Use: Reactivates records which were marked for deletion with the DELETE command.

REINDEX

Syntax: REINDEX

Use: Rebuilds all of the active index files for the current database file.

RELEASE

Syntax: RELEASE <memory variable list> / ALL [LIKE/EXCEPT <skeleton>]

Use: Clears specified memory variables from system memory.

RENAME

Syntax: RENAME <oldname> TO <newname>

Use: Changes the name of the disk file specified by <oldname> to the one specified by <newname>.

REPLACE

Syntax: REPLACE <field(s)> WITH <value> [WHILE <condition>] [FOR <condition>]

Use: Changes the value in a field or fields of selected records in the current database file.

REPORT FORM

Syntax: REPORT FORM <report filename> [WHILE <condition>] [FOR <condition>] [TO PRINT]

Use: Activates a report-format file previously created with the CREATE REPORT or MODIFY REPORT commands.

RESTORE

Syntax: RESTORE FROM <filename> [ADDITIVE]

Use: Loads a set of memory variables from a memory-variable (.MEM) file.

RUN/!

Syntax: RUN <command>
! <command>

Use: Executes a DOS command as though it were typed directly at a DOS prompt.

SAVE

Syntax: SAVE TO <filename> [ALL LIKE/EXCEPT <skeleton>]

Use: Saves memory variables to a .MEM file on disk for later use.

SEEK

Syntax: SEEK <expression>

Use: Searches for the first record in the database file with an index key which matches <expression>.

SELECT

Syntax: SELECT <work area 1–10 / letter *A–J* / alias>

Use: Allows relational and multifile operations by switching between work areas.

SET

Syntax: SET

Use: Enters a menu-driven mode in which the various environmental (SET) commands can be examined and changed.

SET BELL

Syntax: SET BELL ON/OFF

Use: Defines whether *dBase III Plus* should or should not sound a bell when a field becomes filled or when an invalid entry is typed.

SET COLOR

Syntax: SET COLOR TO <standard front/back>,<enhanced front/back>,<border>

Use: Changes the color on color monitors and the screen intensity on monochrome monitors.

SET CONFIRM

Syntax: SET CONFIRM ON/OFF

Use: Determines whether or not the Enter key must be pressed after typing data into full-screen operations such as APPEND or EDIT.

SET CONSOLE

Syntax: SET CONSOLE ON/OFF

Use: Enables or suppresses display to the screen.

SET DECIMALS

Syntax: SET DECIMALS TO <n>

Use: Specifies how many decimal places are displayed with numeric values.

SET DEFAULT TO

Syntax: SET DEFAULT TO <drive>

Use: Specifies which disk drive will be used used for file storage when no particular drive is specified.

SET DELETED

Syntax: SET DELETED ON/OFF

Use: Determines whether records marked for deletion are included in *dBase III* plus commands.

SET DEVICE

Syntax: SET DEVICE TO PRINT/SCREEN

Use: Directs the display of SAY commands to either the printer or the video screen.

SET EXACT

Syntax: SET EXACT ON/OFF

Use: Determines whether partial matches will be accepted when performing string-based comparisons or searches.

SET FIELDS

Syntax: SET FIELDS TO <field list>
SET FIELDS ON/OFF

Use: SET FIELDS TO <field list> specifies a group of fields within the current database file which are to be used in subsequent operations. SET FIELDS ON/OFF activates or deactivates the field list specified in the SET FIELDS TO command.

SET FILTER TO

Syntax: SET FILTER TO <condition>

Use: Causes the database file to appear as though it contains only those records which meet the specified condition.

SET FORMAT TO

Syntax: SET FORMAT TO <format filename>

Use: Activates a format file (.FMT) which controls the screen layout during EDIT and APPEND operations.

SET FUNCTION

Syntax: SET FUNCTION <2–10> TO <expression>

Use: Allows you to redefine the function keys to any desired function.

SET HELP

Syntax: SET HELP ON/OFF

Use: Determines whether *dBase III Plus* offers help automatically whenever a command is entered incorrectly.

SET INDEX TO

Syntax: SET INDEX TO <index filename list>

Use: Activates one or more index files for the current database file.

SET MARGIN

Syntax: SET MARGIN TO <n>

Use: Sets the left margin for all output sent to the printer (default is 0).

SET MEMOWIDTH

Syntax: SET MEMOWIDTH TO <n>

Use: Sets the displayed width of memo fields.

SET ORDER TO

Syntax: SET ORDER TO <n>

Use: Selects which of the active index files (1–7) will control record order.

SET PATH

Syntax: SET PATH TO <pathname>

Use: Instructs *dBase III Plus* where to look for files if they are not found in the current (default) drive and directory.

SET PRINT

Syntax: SET PRINT ON/OFF

Use: Sends output to the printer instead of the screen.

SET PRINTER

Syntax: SET PRINTER TO <device>

Use: Directs printer output to a selected device.

SET RELATION

Syntax: SET RELATION TO <key> INTO <filename>

Use: Establishes relations between two open database files.

SET SAFETY

Syntax: SET SAFETY ON/OFF

Use: Determines whether *dBase III Plus* will display a warning message prior to executing commands which will overwrite or destroy an existing file.

SET STATUS

Syntax: SET STATUS ON/OFF

Use: Determines whether the status display bar will appear on the bottom of the screen.

SET TALK

Syntax: SET TALK ON/OFF

Use: Determines whether the result of interactive operations are displayed on the screen.

SKIP

Syntax: SKIP [<n>]

Use: Moves the record pointer one or more positions forward or backward within the file.

SORT

Syntax: SORT ON <field> TO <filename> [WHILE <condition>] [FOR <condition>]

Use: Creates a new database file with the specified filename from records in the current file, arranged according to the value found in <field>.

SUM

Syntax: SUM <fieldname> [TO <memory variable>] [WHILE <condition>] [FOR <condition>]

Use: Adds the values found in the specified numeric field for those records meeting the optional condition.

USE

Syntax: USE <filename> [INDEX <filename(s)>]

Use: Opens a database file and up to seven index files.

ZAP

Syntax: ZAP

Use: Deletes all records from the active database file.

Index